'This book combines psychoanalytic understanding and a deep knowledge of classical Greek drama. Sotiris Manolopoulos brings out the universal themes in Euripides' play *The Suppliants*, as it explores the relation between past and present, inner and outer, male and female. Central to the book is its discussion, from a psychoanalytic perspective, of political issues. Manolopoulos demonstrates very valuably how *The Suppliants* illuminates the unconscious conflicts involved in maintaining a democratic society.'

– Michael Parsons, *Training Analyst, London*

'A play on Greek society written 2,500 years ago reflecting women, mystery, tragedy, hubris and politics around a core of mourning is a necessary reading for our pandemic times, as broken politics need to be re-imagined.'

– Dr Jonathan Sklar, *Training Analyst, London*

'In an innovative manner, and with an emphasis on the historical and interdisciplinary approach, Sotiris Manolopoulos creates the links between psychoanalytic theory and tragic poetry. In that unique but far-reaching space, the new theorization has been built: about politics as a way of integrating split-off, untranslated and denied elements of mythical acts linked to the process of mourning and the feminine core of existence. This viewpoint is especially important in a time of crisis and transformations, enabling us to learn about the alliances of community, about the connection of psychic and public life, calling for internalization and participation. Many concepts are enlightened and deepened: primary union, work of mourning, feminine core, but also the questions of war and of leadership. The very idea that the foundation of our public life is linked to the integration with the psychic work is appealing, and could be useful for the generations to come'

– Jasminka Šuljagić, *Training Analyst, Psychoanalytical Society of Serbia; General Editor of the European Psychoanalytic Federation*

'This is a book whose time has come. At a moment when we are witnessing the resurgence of political populism, of attacks on science and on truth, and when destructive forces appear to be gaining the upper hand, overriding even man's instinct for self-preservation through denial of the seriousness of a world-wide pandemic and of global climate change, a psychoanalytic understanding of these phenomena of "political hubris" is much needed. We as psychoanalysts struggle to understand what appears to be a recent turn of events, but as Sotiris Manolopoulos points out through his treatise on *Psychoanalysis and Euripides' Suppliant Women*, these are but repetitions of man's struggle to hold "deep unbridgeable contradictions" . . . "impossible links leading to impasses" . . . man's "tragic position". This book will be of interest to psychoanalysts, psychotherapists as well as to students of history, politics and culture. It is well worth reading.'

– Dimitris J. Jackson, *Training Analyst, Hellenic Psychoanalytical Society*

T0299874

Psychoanalysis and Euripides' Suppliant Women

Psychoanalysis and Euripides' Suppliant Women applies the "tragic" reading of politics, presented by Euripides in his play, *The Suppliant Women*, to the contemporary world.

Manolopoulos presents a psychoanalytic assessment of the key themes of the play, considering the phenomenon of hubris in public life indirectly, through its transformation in tragic poetry. *Psychoanalysis and Euripides' Suppliant Women* goes on to consider how the foundations of the polis are linked to the integration of the work of mourning and the feminine core of existence, and how the aims of scholars who study the play correspond to psychoanalysis' work towards understanding the psychic and social reality of politics.

This book allows for a deeper understanding of the pathological modes of mental functioning that manifest in politics. It will be of interest to psychoanalysts in practice and in training and academics and scholars of psychoanalytic studies, politics, and classical studies.

Sotiris Manolopoulos is a member of the Canadian and Hellenic Psychoanalytic Societies, and is a child analyst, training analyst, former director of training and president of the Hellenic Society.

Routledge Focus on Mental Health

Routledge Focus on Mental Health presents short books on current topics, linking in with cutting-edge research and practice.

Single-Session 'One-at-a-Time' Therapy: A Rational Emotive Behaviour Therapy Approach
Windy Dryden

Transforming Performance Anxiety Treatment: Using Cognitive Hypnotherapy and EMDR
Elizabeth Brooker

The Relevance of Rational Emotive Behaviour Therapy for Modern CBT and Psychotherapy
Windy Dryden

An Evidence-based Approach to Authentic Leadership Development
Tony Fusco

Rational Emotive Behaviour Therapy: A Newcomer's Guide
Walter J. Matweychuk and Windy Dryden

Working with Interpreters in Psychological Therapy: The Right to be Understood
Jude Boyles and Nathalie Talbot

Psychoanalysis and Euripides' Suppliant Women: A Tragic Reading of Politics
Sotiris Manolopoulos

Psychoanalysis and Euripides' Suppliant Women

A Tragic Reading of Politics

Sotiris Manolopoulos

Routledge
Taylor & Francis Group

LONDON AND NEW YORK

First published 2022
by Routledge
4 Park Square, Milton Park, Abingdon, Oxon OX14 4RN

and by Routledge
605 Third Avenue, New York, NY 10158

Routledge is an imprint of the Taylor & Francis Group, an informa business

British Library Cataloguing-in-Publication Data
A catalogue record for this book is available from the British Library

Library of Congress Cataloging-in-Publication Data
A catalog record has been requested for this book

ISBN: 978-1-032-17187-6 (hbk)
ISBN: 978-1-032-17186-9 (pbk)
ISBN: 978-1-003-25218-4 (ebk)

DOI: 10.4324/9781003252184

Typeset in Times New Roman
by Apex CoVantage, LLC

To Despoina, Anastasia and Veronica

Contents

Acknowledgements

I would like to thank my colleagues who helped me think and develop the ideas of this book, in particular: Marilia Aisenstein, Dimitris Jackson, Michael Parsons, Jonathan Sklar, Jasminka Šuljagić.

I am grateful to Susannah Frearson who guided me in the process of publication.

I wish to thank Filippos Stylianou for his editorial input.

Permissions acknowledgements

The 13 lines of the poem (Seferis. G. (1995). MYCENAE, Oct. 1935. In George Seferis *Collected Poems-Revised Edition*, Translated, edited and introduced by Edmund Keeley and Philip Sherrard, Princeton: Princeton University Press, cited in this book, are reprinted by kind permission of Princeton University Press.

Also, the same lines of the poem (Seferis. G. (1995). II MYCENAE, Oct. 1935. In George Seferis *Complete Poems*, trans Edmund Keeley and Philip Sherrard. London: Carcanet Classics) cited in this book are reprinted by kind permission of Carcanet Press, Manchester, UK.

Foreword

Sotiris Manolopoulos, a psychoanalyst and man of letters, offers us a political, psychoanalytic, and philosophical view of this superb tragedy of Euripides.

The author immediately sees in the tragedy the drama of the human being confronted from childhood with the loss of his dream of omnipotence, and who, in order to become a subject, must gain access to ambivalence and uncertainty. Furthermore, in order to become a thinking subject, a subjective being, he will have to renounce triumphant narcissism and accept that he must experience interiority and bisexuality.

The plot of the play oscillates between logos and pathos. Its end is a dramatic one. The tragedy takes place in front of the temple of Demeter in Eleusis; the mother of Theseus, Aithra, is approached by the mothers of Argos warriors who died during the battle of the "Seven against Thebes" and were deprived of burials. Adrastus, king of Argos, mourns with the mothers in tears. He asks for help from Theseus, king of Athens, who finally accepts; Theseus leaves for Thebes with his army, but without Adrastus so as not to create any ambiguity between the recovery of the bodies and the attempted invasion of Argos during the War of the Seven.

Theseus returns with the bodies of the warriors which are cremated together. The orphans of the warriors bring the ashes of their fathers to their grandmothers with promises of revenge. The Argives admit to Theseus that they owe a debt to Athens but Athena, who considers that this is not enough, appears on the roof of the temple and asks Theseus to make Adrastus promise that he will never attack Athens. Finally, Athena announces to the children that they will avenge their fathers and sack the city of Thebes.

As in all his tragedies Euripides uses the framework of the mythological account of the war of the Seven against Thebes to analyse through a dialogue the virtues of the two great political systems of ancient Greece: democracy and tyranny.

I would like to add here that *The Seven against Thebes*, Aeschylus' tragedy, the story of which takes place before *The Suppliants*, relates the fratricidal war between Eteocles and Polynices, sons of Oedipus, for the possession of the city of Thebes. Thebes is saved but the two brothers die.

Their uncle Creon decides that Polynices' corpse will be abandoned without burial and left in the sun. He has the body watched by guards and announces the death penalty for anyone who offers a burial for the body. But Antigone, his sister, decides on her own to give him a decent burial.

The play ends with the lamentations of the choir.

I would remind the reader that Antigone is the subject of two tragedies by Sophocles: *Oedipus at Colonus,* where we see her guiding her blind and sick father through Attica, and the *Antigone* that we all know.

Like Greek mythology, Greek tragedy is an infinite succession of incest, murders and fratricidal hatreds, culminating in the Oresteia of Aeschylus and his last play *The Eumenides* where we see Orestes grappling with the Furies (Erinyes, for whom the Eumenides is a euphemism, the Erinyes symbolizing the remorse and pain of the matricide which drives Orestes mad).

Sotiris Manolopoulos invites us to imagine being spectators and seeks to deepen our psychoanalytic knowledge. We are silent and attentive; we will discover the different forms of hubris, the insolence of man, which are punished by the Gods.

This is told through scenes so well described that the reader feels he is on the steps of an ancient theatre, that of Epidaurus perhaps.

Sotiris Manolopoulos also quotes Jaqueline de Romilly[1] who wrote that Euripides examined time in relation to human feelings that bring a disorder in his plots. Time is of an emotional order. Talking about time the persons talk about their emotions. She notices that there is often impatience and relief, a sense of "at last". The theatrical unexpected act at the last moment saves the situation and makes the passions rise to extreme intensity.

It is interesting to note that the tragedy begins with a woman, Aithra, taking the place of the goddess of peace Demeter, who rediscovers her daughter after the latter's return from Hades, and ends with another woman, the goddess of war Athena, who takes the place of Evadne who is forever lost in Hades.

Struggling with his demons, the human being seeks how to institute laws and order which can integrate, without any exclusions, myths and religion within a moderate democracy. Euripides provides us here with a diagnosis of the human condition; he notes a split between the field of consciousness and the forces which elude us and move us independently of our will.

In Greek Antiquity, the hero was subject to his fate, so he had to accept it, but with dignity. Through his tragedies, Euripides pleads for a human society capable of accepting imperfection and uncertainty. He makes a significant distinction, for psychoanalysts, between two kinds of shame: the "good" kind that we call guilt and the "bad" kind that we would call shame because it is on the side of narcissism and not of the superego.

Theseus is a tragic hero who has an important place in Greek Mythology. He is above all a hero of Attica and as a teenager, he overcame all his trials, returning victorious at the age of 16 to Athens. The affairs of the city were at that time in a state of extreme confusion. There followed the war of the Amazons and the well-known episode of the Minotaur and also the inglorious abandonment of Ariadne to Naxos, from which Richard Strauss drew inspiration for a sublime opera.

Under the reign of Theseus, Athens prospered; he made it a capital, endowed it with a Council (*βουλή*), a Prytaneion, organised the "Panathenaean" festivals, a symbol of political unity, coined money, and so on. He showed himself to be a true statesman, firm and wise. I would add here that it was he who allowed Oedipus to die and to be buried in a secret place in Attica.

Sotiris Manolopoulos' reading of the *Suppliants* subtly transmits to us the psychoanalytical and "political" dimension of Euripides's tragedy. He underlines the struggle of a Polis in order to survive human's hate and destructivity.

We have to understand that the polis represents a body of society with an unknown hidden space full of mysterious processes whereby everyday life interactions take place. In order to be in contact with this secret internal space and to support its development, we need the transitional phenomena of religion, poetry and politics, which make a movement geared towards an objective. Though this growth is always disappointing because orations are obscure and the incomprehensible unknown forces that are compulsively repeated and shake the very foundations of the "Polis". Human beings want to know, to understand, and to control. And they have to realise that they do not know, do not understand.

For us psychoanalysts, politics and ethics are linked with the question of the "superego". Both prohibiting and protective, the latter is made up of the identifications with the superegos of both the parents and grandparents. In the Greek world complexity lies in the question of identifications; the Gods are omnipotent and identifying with them is a matter of hubris.

The Suppliants ends with Athena, the goddess of war, but also of wisdom, inviting the Athenians to create alliances; she urges them to concentrate on the the art of politics which makes it possible to link external reality and our internal phantasy scenarios. This is the only way to become subjects who are capable of opposing each other as well as of uniting and creating meaning.

In my opinion, Sotiris Manolopoulos' analysis of Euripes' tragedy is truly remarkable for he tackles the difficult task of intertwining the veins of psychoanalytical, sociological, and political reflection. He manages to do this thanks to a deep knowledge of psychoanalytic theory, but also an impressive multidisciplinary culture along with a great deal of talent and humanism.

Marilia Aisenstein
Paris, Kirinthos Euboea October 28, 2021

Note

1 Jacqueline de Romilly Le Temps dans la Tragédie Grecque, 1972, Editions Vrin

Introduction

Let us imagine that we are the audience of Euripides'[1] political play *Suppliant Women*. We rely on the poet's tragic reading of politics to widen our psychoanalytic understanding. Today, we are concerned about the many faces of hubris in public life. So, we attend in silence, anticipating being surprised by the innovations that Euripides introduces to the myth of the Suppliants. We subject ourselves to the tragic effects of the play.

In *Suppliant Women*, politics is read in a democratic polis as the struggle of humans to establish the rule of law and integrate – not replace – primitive mythical beliefs and religious and mystical acts. This is Euripides' painful diagnosis of the human condition: Men are deeply split. They struggle to integrate split-off divine, wild, "supernatural" forces and limits that lie beyond the order of politics, words, and reason. Psychoanalysis calls them the unconscious. This struggle takes a dramatic course in a crisis, when the polis is in transition and in need to re-invent its identity.

In *Suppliant Women*, politics is the struggle of humans to integrate irreducible split-off elements of mythical religious acts and beliefs that are linked to processes of mourning and the feminine core of existence. These elements lend the weight of historical truth and convincing reality to the inscription of modern written laws and the founding of institutions. By integrating these elements, politics enables humans to negotiate alliances of community, sustain participation in common culture, construct a shared reality, and allow an open-ended process of transformations to continue.

Euripides presents a complex political vision of a complicated world, where people struggle to withstand reality and construct its multiple meanings with words and actions, which connect them to other speaking subjects in the public domain. He advocates the acceptance of an imperfect society. Only fanaticism and paranoia make things simple. People have beliefs and ideals towards which they strive. Their struggles are never conclusive enough because human lives follow unexpected turns brought about by irrational forces.

DOI: 10.4324/9781003252184-1

The tragedian presents on stage of the man's[2] struggles to face the shock of the loss of omnipotence as he leaves the primary union and moves towards becoming a separate autonomous subject. He introduces the plot of a story, a transitional reality between the mental and the social, which the subject has to cross. The plot of the tragedy transforms the impossible impasses caused by splitting into paradoxes, which humans can tolerate. It aims at keeping the tension up and the play open-ended thus maintaining the integration processes of being and thinking.

In breaking away from the primary union, humans emerge as tragic subjects who put on the "yoke of necessity",[3] submitting personally to the inescapable secret will of age-long mysterious forces. This means that they undertake as subjects the responsibility to give meaning and integrate the experiences they perform on the stage of everyday life.

Euripides realises, as psychoanalysis does, that humans hate restrictions imposed by the meaning-giving and integration processes and seek the primitive pleasure afforded them by the annihilating attack on any line of resistance, order, and organisation of the object and the thinking processes.

Euripides' *Suppliant Women* listen to the dark depths of human nature, the source of destructive fratricidal violence, as Thucydides discovered. Freud (1932) also tried to answer the question "why war?" Today we struggle to find our orientation in a bewildered world and fear that we will become irrelevant. We often resort to hubris: war, tyranny, fakery, populism, cruelty, fanaticism, racism, and misogyny.

In *Suppliant Women* humans yoke the necessity to represent and integrate (internalise, subjectivise) to the order of politics their drives, omnipotence, and bisexuality, as these are expressed in the passions of mourning and femininity, which lie beyond any order of words or reason. A tragic plot begins to unravel when the subjects dare go down the painful path of internalising this necessity in their psychic and public life. They become its tragic subjects.

The modern democratic polis is based on the rule of law. The tragic poet is the modern prophet needed for the politics of the democratic polis.

Notes

1 In spelling Greek names and words, I follow The Cambridge Greek Lexicon (2021). This is a compromise between keeping the Latinisation of familiar names and words and using a precise transliteration.
2 In this book I have tried to avoid sexist language. Sometimes I use "he" or "his" to refer to subjects of either sex for the sake of simplicity.
3 Aeschylus' Agamemnon, cited in Williams (1993).

References

The Cambridge Greek Lexicon (2021) Vols. 1 & 2. Cambridge, Cambridge University Press.

Freud S. (1932) Why War? *S.E., 22*.

Williams B. (1993) *Shame and Necessity*. Berkeley and Los Angeles, University of California Press.

1 The plot

Sotiris Manolopoulos

Aithra, the mother of the young King of Athens, Theseus, stands silent at the centre of the orchestra in front of the altar of the two goddesses, Demeter and her daughter Persephone (Kore). She has left the secure privacy of her home and come to Eleusis to offer sacrifice and burn gifts at the public ritual of Proerosia, the Panhellenic festival of fertility in late October, for the first fruits of the year's harvest. Suddenly a chorus of grieving women appear, bearing boughs of supplication, which they place on the ground encircling Aithra.

As the aged woman honours peacefully and silently the fertility rite in this land of mysteries, she is confronted by the uncanny entreaty. Aithra finally speaks and utters her prologue. She positions herself as the subject of her words and deeds. She is placed within time and space. This is what she says: The Suppliants are the grey-haired mothers of the Seven Generals from Argos who had marched against Thebes. They were all defeated and killed before its gates. They fought alongside Polyneikes against his brother Eteokles. Both brothers were killed in battle, fulfilling the curse of their father Oedipus. Creon their uncle, the new King of Thebes, banned the burial of the Seven.

The mothers together with the sons of the Seven and the old King Adrastos of Argos, have come to Eleusis to find Aithra and beg her to intercede with her son Theseus, King of Athens, in persuading Creon to give them their perished sons to bury. It is a matter of necessity, an existential need.

> Not reverent, I come, but driven
>
> by need (64–66)[1]

We are situated at Eleusis, the holy place where Demeter is the guardian of the hearth. Eleusis is the place where Demeter lost her daughter, Kore, abducted by the death-god Hades, thus causing the mother to wander incessantly in a mournful search for her. This is the place where Kore every year

DOI: 10.4324/9781003252184-2

returns for some months to live with her earth-mother and generate newborn life. Demeter is the goddess of the earth from where life springs forth and in the dark depths of which the dead and their secrets are buried. Her name means earth-mother (*De-meter, Δη-μήτηρ*). Demeter is a mother. The Athenians believed themselves to be autochthonous (*αὐτόχθονες*), indigenous, who were born of the land itself.

At the land of Eleusis arrive the Suppliants, childless mothers like Demeter. The verb i*kneomai* (*ἱκνέομαι*), means to arrive at, make one's way, reach, supplicate, plead, beg, come upon (a state of grief, longing, anger, fatigue, hunger) come about, and appropriate. From the same root are also derived the words able (*ikanos, ἱκανός*), trace (*ichnos, ἴχνος*), attainable (*efiktos, ἐφικτός*), and fitting (The Cambridge Greek Lexicon, 2021:707).[2]

When the Suppliants arrive at Eleusis their tragic plot begins to unfold. It brings to the present the traces of the past and the seeds of the actions that anticipate the future. A story begins from a position that the hero has achieved; a place to stand and make his way, to create and find his objects. We can think of a tragic position which is achieved when one separates from the primary union, he lives the shock of the loss of omnipotence and creates an internal space where he integrates his experiences he lives and becomes their subject.

The first innovation of Euripides' tragic plot is the role of Aithra

The Eleusinian holy "nursery" of newborn life is now filled with "ghosts", unburied war dead. With their branches of supplication and beating their breasts, the lamenting mothers surround Aithra. "Bound, but not bound, by boughs" she then waits there by the altars of the goddesses [30–32]. She calls for her son to come and free her and the city from the boughs of supplication. One of Euripides' greatest visionary characters, Aithra, is deeply moved. She takes pity on the Suppliants and she responds with a sense of religious urgency (Scully, 1995:7).

We are in the middle of a crisis. The supplication has suddenly disturbed the religious settings of the sacred institutions, making them acutely perceived as real. Already, mysterious wild "supernatural" elements are released. We can think that these are untranslated elements of a personal and shared past. They cannot be eradicated or remembered in words. They can only be experienced, suffered and countered with actions or become split-off, denied and evacuated.

> discharge our obligation through some deed
> the gods approve
>
> [37–38].

Aithra invites her son to appear in public, to "be born" alive on stage. She expects him to enter a path that has already been initiated, to become a leader.

The political supplication asks of him to make (constrained by his own and the city's true character) a free and critical decision of vital importance for himself and for the state for which he is responsible (Zuntz, 1955:6).

In response to his fear that the supplication is a threat to his city, Theseus' first reaction is a harsh criticism against the older King of Argos. He forcefully refuses to help Adrastos, because he had without prudence sent his army to destruction. He had shown no respect for the divine omens. He had discarded reason and married his two daughters off to foreigners, two beasts, Polyneikes and Tydeus.

Theseus' argument is conclusive but incomplete (Zuntz, 1955:7). Timing is crucial. Aithra intervenes. She tells Theseus that he must above all keep in mind the gods and the Panhellenic laws – an order of the larger world. Heroic courage is required in order to take civil action and gain personal honour and civil glory. He has the future to think of; the pride for the future integration of himself and his city. He has to identify himself with his polis. He is to become who he is, the son of Aithra, a man.

> My son, first, and foremost, it's the will of gods
> you have to consider
>
> [298–299].

> . . .
>
> you wouldn't want it said that you hung back,
> afraid, when you could have wrested the crown
> of fame for your city
>
> [311–13].

> . . .
>
> My son, if you are indeed
> my son, don't shame yourself
>
> [316–317]

Aithra persuades Theseus to change his mind. A mother urges her son to identify with his father and become a man. The key words here are "courage" and "shame". The bold youth, who hunts wild beasts and wins contests all over Greece, is helped by his mother to enter a path of identification and transformation, embark on a struggle to mature and become a leader, defender of the divine and human law.

Storey (2008:38) observes: "Aithra occupies the central dramatic focus of the theatre. . . . Theseus has been in the wrong dramatic space, talking to the wrong dramatic character. Pity, rather than self-righteous condemnation is his proper response". The Seven had been severely punished by their deaths for the wrong they did. They do not have to be deprived of their burial. By not burying the dead, Creon deprives them of the right to belong to the human canon.

We sense the awe and the fear on stage leading to sympathy towards the suffering mothers and anger against the reckless men of Argos. Theseus tells Adrastos with contempt: "And am I to become your ally?"

At first Theseus ignores the respect and shame (aidos, αἰδώς) owed to others and to justice (dike, δίκη) according to the human and divine law that ordains the dead should be buried. He embarrasses us. In his Hippolytos Crowned, Euripides distinguishes between good and bad shame. Good shame (aidos, αἰδώς) guides one to respect justice; it stems from the gaze of the others that makes one a subject of one's community. The bad shame (*aishyne, αἰσχύνη*) carries with it the heavy burden of devaluation; it ostracises one from one's house and community (Manolopoulos, 1999:187).

Williams (1993:146) studied shame and necessity both in Homer and tragic poets along with Thucydides. Tragedies contain the idea of necessity that stems from supernatural processes, which lie beyond the logical conception of nature and beyond the meaning which humans construct, and the culture they share. Eteokles, in Aeschylus' *Seven against Thebes*, is the first tragic subject. He knows what will happen when next morning he goes to face his brother Polyneikes at the seventh gate of Thebes. And yet he has to personally take over – be the subject of – his fate. The tragic subject is a hero who personally accepts not to escape but to suffer his fate, which has been ordained by divine mysterious forces since long ago.

Theseus finally makes his decision based on justice. He neither supports the reckless Argives' war nor opposes the tyranny of Thebes. He acts according to shame. He thinks: What will those who hate him say if his own mother asks him to undertake this labour and he refuses?

Here begins Theseus' adventure of discovering and inventing the world. Initially he enjoys the logical face-to-face confrontation, whereby a mirror of reality is held up to him that makes him see through the eyes of the other. Gradually, he learns to respect the invisible forces that are active out of his control, plunge the political order into chaos and turn the mirror upside down.

Nothing good in human affairs lasts forever; God overturns things. No one can ignore the unknown. No one escapes the supernatural divine forces and limits.

We now watch Theseus, the tragic hero, put himself under the yoke of necessity, under a regime of integration. He moves off stage into the orchestra to join hands with his mother and take the lead. He frees her from the supplication and leaves for Athens, a place of politics. He starts his campaign by addressing the citizens of Athens, convincing them democratically to embrace the cause of the Argives. He then prepares an army in order to seize the dead by force if the Thebans are not persuaded to surrender them peacefully.

The labours of the heroic subject like those of the city become one in Theseus' transformations. This is a common (koinon) labour that makes a community out of separate subjects. Theseus does not deny what he had said in the beginning. He still thinks that Adrastos has been hubristic by discarding reason and showing disrespect to the gods. But he repeats what his mother taught him. He begins to widen his awareness and ours:

> Now let the corpses be hidden in the earth
> from which each came to light; let soul release
> to air, body to earth. We do not own
> our bodies, but we are tenants there for life
> and earth that nursed them takes back again

[517–521].

The necessity of war is the second innovation of Euripides

The Herald then enters and arrogantly presents the Thebans' audacious demands. He inserts the logic of the inevitable conflict that leads to war.[3] Theseus defends Athens, and democracy. Athens is a free city. All people are equal before the law [427]. Equality guarantees individual life and common security. Athens is praised for defending ethics and the universal rule of law. If Creon does not accept to peacefully cede the dead, Athens will go to war.

Are these principles worth fighting and dying for? This is what Euripides puts to the test (Zuntz, 1955:17). In his *Suppliants*, war results from the inability of men who desire peace to achieve it by rational deliberation. In Aeschylus' *Seven against Thebes* the dead are retrieved through the power of persuasion.[4] Euripides puts new questions: Why is war necessary? When is a war just?

Theseus' argument with the Theban Herald begins as a formal debate and in the end degenerates into one-line exchanges with insults. They do not counter each other's arguments. Their agon is like any other game to win. It ends with no compromise. You have your opinion and I have mine. Theseus accuses the Herald of stupidly wasting words. Scully (1995:9) believes that the self-conscious repetitions and reversals are deliberate, designed to reveal the inability of words to settle certain hostilities.

THESEUS: leave our land, pack up your empty words.
It's pointless talking

[564–565]

This deep poetic insight helps us to understand politics as the struggle to bridge the irreducible splits, which are inherent in humans and their polis.

Before the walls of Thebes war is inevitable. Unless Creon changes his mind, spears will speak. Creon remains silent when at the last moment the Athenians offer him peace. The same happened, as Adrastos painfully recalls, when the Seven took the field. Eteokles offered them peace but Adrastos had rejected it. It is useless. Words and reason do not provide adequate limits to the forces of destruction.

The Messenger enters and brings the news anxiously awaited: The Athenians fought and won. The Messenger introduces a geographically and temporally distant and heroic epic past. He describes Thebes with its "formidable seven gates", the "epic-like battle" and a "warrior Theseus, who provides the mythic foundation for Athens' superiority". Then he moves on to a theatrical here-and-now. "An escaped Argive prisoner of war, the Messenger watches the battle like a thrilled theatregoer, shouting, applauding . . ., and dancing his approval of the Athenian victory" (Rhem, 2002:27).

The gruesome reality of the uncompromised contradictions and violence of war are presented by the Messenger as choreography.

A dazzling blade of sunlight, a clear rod,
Struck the earth . . . . . .
I saw it all, I didn't just hear of it –
. . . Core against core, the armies slammed together;
They butchered and were butchered, and with great cries

[623–667]

Then the Messenger praises Theseus who stopped before the walls though he could pass through them and sack the city of Thebes. Theseus becomes a true leader (brave but with limited ambition) as the plot unfolds. The general we elect must be brave in adversity and despise *hubristic people* (*hubristēn laon*, ὑβριστήν λαόν) who are unable to maintain their happiness because arrogantly they cannot wait and want to immediately escalate a situation.

"Scaling the top of the ladder as a metaphor for overreaching ambitions inevitably evokes Kapaneus, one of the seven leaders of the expedition against Thebes". He had climbed the ladder to conquer the Theban walls. His blasphemous boasts provoked Zeus "to topple him from the ladder with a lightning bolt". Thus, he was made the 'emblem of hubris'" (Burian, 1985:144).

Theseus did not give in to the populist demands of arrogant people.

We did not come to destroy
the city', he cried, but to rescue the dead

[689–690]

To rescue the dead! The Athenian army brings the corpses of the Seven back to Eleusis, burns them on a pyre and delivers the ashes to their sons. One, that of Capaneus – the sacred of the Seven because he was struck by Zeus with a lightning bolt – is burned in a separate pyre prepared by Theseus.

Theseus appropriates the women's cultural right and performs the funeral rites for him and for the city. He even washes the bodies of the dead himself. In this way he shows to the Athenians that they should not be afraid of the dead bodies. Then he asks Adrastos to deliver the funeral oration. He sees in the obsequies the opportunity to teach the young what virtue means.

The villain of the myth will be an example of virtue. The young can learn something from the dead even now, even from their death. There is a chance to create and share an experience and learn from it. They will learn to weave links of identifications, to reinforce the bonds that form a society, a "koinonia" ("koinon", common). Euripides questions the establishment and inserts irony and tension into the way things are in reality and the way we represent them in our stories. The pain brings us all figuratively together, in a union.

Universality of pathos: the third innovation

Then, completely unexpected and unannounced the most daring episode of Evadne's suicide, with its savage emotionality, takes place before our eyes, in a burning present moment. The bride of the hubristic Capaneus, daughter of Iphis, sister of one of the Seven, enters from a cliff overlooking Eleusis above the stage. Dressed in white clothes she announces her intention to leap from the cliff into her husband's pyre. Like a bird she stands on the *airy rock (aitheria petra, αἰθερία πέτρα)* and hovers over the stage, ready to escape to freedom, to fly to death.

EVADNE: What torchlight, what brilliant glare
Did sun and moon drive through the air

[945–946]

. . .

I've rushed here from my house
like a Maenad running loose

to see the pyre's light and the holy tomb,
and to lead my soul
from life's long toil
into death's great room
death is voluptuous,
to die with our lovers

[953–960]

Evadne's father Iphis rushes from Argos, searching for his daughter who escaped from the paternal house after having returned there, as she was wont to do after the death of her husband Capaneus. Like the grieving mothers, Iphis despairs that he would neither have a son nor a daughter.

Mothers and fathers now only look forward to their own death, to nothingness.

IPHIS; Go home? And see that echoing void
In room after room, my whole life out of place?
. . .
Lead me away and shut me in the dark,
and let my old body melt away without food

[1048–1056]

The hushed sons of the Seven dead generals now dramatically break their silence. In the end of the play, it is the sons and not the weary mothers who hold their noble fathers' bodies (bones and ashes) in their hands. They will shoulder the burden of avenging each their fathers' deaths.

CHILDREN: I bear them, I bear them-
Sad mother, I bear my father's bones from the flame.
So heavy they are, woe weighted with grief, my whole
In a jar so small.

[1074–1077]

Athena, yet another woman, knows the end of the story

The tragedy does not end when Theseus and Adrastos exchange words acknowledging mutual debt and promises for future alliance. Words and reason are not enough. Athena comes forth to teach the Athenians a lesson in politics. She instructs Theseus not to rely on words and reason only but also to base the alliance between Athens and Argos on the solemn undertaking by the Argives that no matter what, they will always help Athens whenever faced with danger. This is what alliance of community means. Athenians act on their words and they should demand the same from their allies. Alliance means unbroken link between words and actions.

Theseus is instructed to cut the throats of three lambs in the bronze tripod, which Herakles had left in Athens after his return from Troy. He had pledged Theseus to set it up in Delphi. Theseus should inscribe the oaths of the Argives in the hollow basin of the tripod. Then he should offer it to Apollo at Delphi in order to preserve the memory of it. The knife used for the sacrifice should then be buried in the earth by the site of the pyres of the Seven. The knife would guard the land and fight against whoever might attack it. We can remember now that the dead are also buried in the womb of the earth and have become seeds of vengeance, which will grow in due time.

> Athena tells him . . . that another kind of logos is needed . . . an oath to be broken at incalculable peril. For the *memory* (*mnēmēn, μνήμην*) on which Theseus relies Athena substitutes the concrete *token* (*mnēmeia, μνημεῖα*) of a bronze tripod . . . to be "set up in Delphi as an unchanging witness of what happened there.
>
> (Burian, 1985:153)

Athena finally proclaims that the sons of the Seven will be called Epigonoi. These sons will go to war and destroy Thebes and avenge their fathers' deaths when they grow up. Aigialeus, the son of Adrastos, will lead a mighty army; their fame will resound in songs; they will march with the god. They will be given immortality in songs.

The tragedy begins with a woman Aithra taking the place of the goddess of peace, Demeter, who rediscovers her daughter after the latter's return from Hades, and ends with another woman, the goddess of war, Athena, who takes the place of Evadne for ever lost in Hades. This is how the play unfolds.

Notes

1 All direct line quotes from here on are taken from the translation of Rosanna Warren and Stephen Scully (Euripides' Suppliant Women, 1995). It is part of the series in which the tragic poets are translated only by poets.
2 Throughout this book I rely on the etymology of Greek words as a source of rich associations.
3 Thucydides (1.23) explained the logic of the destined war; what made war inevitable was the rise of Athenian power and the fear this caused to Sparta.
4 Herodotus wrote that "we took the field against the Thebans, recovered the bodies, and laid them to rest in our territory at Eleusis" (Storey, 2008:15).

References

Burian P. (1985) Logos and Pathos: The Politics of the Suppliant Women. In P. Burian (Ed.) *Directions in Euripidean Criticism: A Collection of Essays*. Durham, NC, Duke University Press.

Cambridge University Press, Faculty of Classics. (2021) *The Cambridge Greek Lexicon*. Vols. 1 & 2. Cambridge, Cambridge University Press.

Euripides'. (1995) *Suppliant Women*. (Trans. R. Warren and S. Scully). Oxford, Oxford University Press.

Manolopoulos S. (1999) 'Euripides' Hippolytus: The Familiar Things. *Psychoanalytic Studies*, *1*(2), 177–189.

Rhem R. (2002) *The Play of Space: Spatial Transformation in Greek Tragedy*. Princeton and Oxford, Princeton Universities Press.

Scully S. (1995) Introduction. In *Euripides' Suppliant Women*. (Trans. Rosanna Warren and Stephen Scully). Oxford, Oxford University Press.

Storey C. (2008) *Euripides: Suppliant Women*. London, Duckworth.

Thucydides'. (1910) *The Peloponnesian War*. London, J. M. Dent; New York, E. P. Dutton.

Williams B. (1993) *Shame and Necessity*. Berkeley and Los Angeles, University of California Press.

Zuntz G. (1955) *The Political Plays of Euripides*. Manchester, Manchester University Press.

2   The tragic position

Sotiris Manolopoulos

The *Suppliants* is one of Euripides' two political plays (the other is *The Children of Herakles*). It mirrors political realities of the time it was first staged, around 424 BC. It is a political play in the sense that it uses as its artistic material the problems of human fellowship. In this sense it is ecumenical (Zuntz, 1955).

Burian (1985:129) argues: "This play, more than any other in the canon, cries out for political interpretation, and it has received many". Some interpretations tried to isolate politics *in* the play in order to dig out a message of adherence to some contemporary faction or figure. "It is the politics *of* the play that demands attention, the politics encoded in the structure of its discourse . . . its political codes". What Euripides perceives in his world, influences his choices of expression. However, his choices are made for internal reasons. "In the last analysis, we take Euripides seriously as a political thinker only if we take him seriously as a dramatist".

I agree with those who believe that the *Suppliant Women* is a profound and moving but neglected masterpiece. The play holds a mirror up to reflect politics in a moderate democratic society. It does not just give us material for interpretation. It constitutes a political "working through" of conflicts and traumas. It reflects the polis' struggle to recognise and deal with primitive split-off elements. These are inadequately represented and integrated elements of mourning and femininity inherent in men and their polis.

Euripides makes a moving comment on his polis' struggles, woes and greatness. He probably wrote *The Suppliants* around 424 B.C., seven years after the start of the Peloponnesian War. That same year the Athenians were negotiating with the Thebans over the recovery of their dead from the recent battle of Delium.

We may remind ourselves that not long before, in 429–430 B.C., Athenians suffered a massive trauma, a devastating epidemic, in which one in four people died by a horrible contagious disease. Their leader Perikles died

DOI: 10.4324/9781003252184-3

of it. Thucydides (Book 2, Chapter 52), who was also infected, wrote: "All the burial rites before in use were entirely upset and they buried the bodies as best they could". This meant a major disruption in the continuity of culture.

Euripides does not refer to the epidemic. We can think, however, that its devastating consequences influenced his expressive choices. In an epidemic the mourning rites are entirely upset. The daily threat against life does not leave room for mourning work. Early traumas are activated. People avoid being subjects of the experience of time; they lose the tragic sense of transience.

In the *Suppliants* the mourning rites are disrupted by hubris and the fertility rites are upset by the supplication. Euripides presents democracy as not affected irreparably by the epidemics. It continues to function and develop its rule of law that preserves the coherence (*sunehein, συνέχειν*) of the polis. Individuals and the polis need to share an illusion of immortality in order to bear the threat of an imminent reality.

There is a paranoid need – deeply seated in the foundations of the polis – to control order and organise communication. It stems from the efforts for integration and the fear of disintegration, a threat of horizontal abolition of the differentiating boundaries of laws. Drama, like democracy, recognises the omnipotent arrogance that abolishes limits and differences. It struggles with the horizontal threat (like epidemics) of the hubris of tyranny and the populism of demagogues. Both tyrants and populist demagogues abuse the language and distort the reality of the external object. They stir up pathos that attack the links of logos and actions. They then offer protection to people from their own threats.

Drama and democracy create space where the myth meets the logos that integrates the primitive elements. They uphold the processes of development – comparable to those that a child undergoes under the good enough maternal care – in which the ego acquires the capacity to make the object external, objective. The object is attacked violently by destructive drives, survives, and is placed out there to be used. The ego becomes a subject that can use the object for internalisation in order to learn from the experience (Winnicott, 1971:89).

An epidemic reminds us that nature is infinite. You do not feel castrated by nature. You feel devastated, crushed or elevated, exalted. Perhaps war is the struggle of man to transform the passive experience of a massive trauma into an active repetition. Man strives in a state of extreme helplessness to create a mental object, that is, something or someone whose loss would be meaningful to him. He tries belatedly to become a subject of the traumatic experience of the trauma, to be able to think and have the responsibility of making choices.

We may surmise that the unthinkable anxiety of one being expelled from the world of the living and going to a world of shadows, the body disintegrating, in the play is defended against with the compulsion to repeat the antagonisms in the agora and in the war, where there is movement and resistance, mourning and joy, time, and object relationships, in short life. The loss of the object means the annihilation of self at a deep level of mental life.

Euripides' *Suppliant Women* is dominated by the dead (Rhem, 1992). Corpses, funerals, and mourners fill the stage in a place of Eleusinian mysteries dedicated to the conquest of death. At the same time, the play is a celebratory reminder to Athenians of their city's "finest hour". Ordinary mortals "rescue" their dead from a wretched death and secure their immortality. They mourn them properly. They remember them. They use their memory against death.

The play is also dominated by argumentations, words, reason, rhetoric and poetics of politics, an effort to overcome the agony of extinction. It takes place within boundaries defined by the transgressive movements of women. Courageous women dare make their entrances and attempt heroic exits from their traps.

Considering all possibilities

The critics note that his two political plays (*The Suppliant Women, The Children of Herakles*) are not paradoxically referred to as a source of insightful thinking about politics. The *Suppliant Women* is not frequently performed. Actors, directors, or scholars do not find it an attractive play. Some dismiss it because of its plot, which is seen as odd, unsatisfactory, incoherent and incomprehensible. Some episodes are out of place or overblown, just to lengthen the text, or perhaps as a reply to his critics.

Grube (1941:240) thinks that in *Suppliants* the propagandist got the better of the dramatist, the result being both hasty and careless. Some scenes are quite unworthy and have probably suffered textual tampering. The contemporary reference to the debate on democracy strains the epic framework to an unusual extent. The Evadne episode is not worked adequately into the play. Aithra and Evadne are considered to be of minor importance. For Kitto (1961) this tragedy causes uneasiness and embarrassment. It is a play of national propaganda. The topical nature of the whole is unusually obvious.

However, we should remind ourselves that an everyday familiar speech is often used in Euripides' tragic plots. The ordinary people, the gallery of the theatre, come on stage and cause an uncanny familiarity, an alarming contemporaneity. These subversive plots express open critical thinking. Their endings are unresolved.

Euripides' plays are full of contradictions, surprises, subversive reversals, and unexpected overthrows. They bring the future with an astonishing plausibility and a traumatic perceptual accuracy. They mirror the incoherence, the cacophony, of everyday life. They do not round up the edges. These daring dramaturgies stage the traumatic violent return of the split-off elements, beyond meaning, which lead the plot to an impasse and make necessary an exodos via the intervention of Deus ex Machina.

Storey (2008:104) thinks that "Perhaps Euripides' own comic clone gives its best in Aristophanes' Frogs 954–7: 'I taught them . . . to perceive, to look, to dodge artfully, to be subtle, to suspect the worst, to consider all possibilities'. He certainly succeeded in Suppliant Women".

Knox (1985:5–7) interpreted the world of Euripides "as one of disruption, violence, subversion, uncertainty, discord". The poet's keen vision cut him off from his fellow citizens. "He saw beyond" like a prophet. The prophets in the Bible wrote on the wall words that the King could not understand.

> Euripidean tragedy is the writing on the Athenian wall. It measures and weighs, understands and pities. It does not condemn, for the situation is beyond judgment; it does not propose reform, for it is beyond action. Euripides attempts to understand and to sympathise, but he offers no comfort, no solution, no explanation, only sympathy.

Euripides rescues the myths from censorship. Green (1980) remarks: With the passage of time, the more the myth of Theseus becomes integrated, the more it is censored, rationalised and personalised, becoming a vehicle for moralising memory. The biographer Plutarch – he was no poet – tries to talk about Theseus as if he were a historical persona. To the contrary, the tragic poet teaches us to respect the unknown forces, which transfer on to the theatre stage of everyday life split off early and traumatic unassimilated experiences and the weight of their historical truth.

"Off subject"

The plot of *Suppliant Women* oscillates between logos and pathos. Its closure is a difficult one. Evadne gives a dramatic end that seals the sorrow of the grieving mothers. Athena gives the end that seals the logos of Theseus.

We do not have a solid ground on which to stand. Every allusion to the ethics of the play is contradicted by an opposite one. A dramatic episode suddenly occupies the public space. And then it is forgotten. The play continues as if Evadne's dramatic suicide never happened. As soon as Adrastos finishes his fine didactic funeral oration, the mothers sing in nine powerful lines their devastating personal loss. The mothers suffer and display their despair. The sons of the dead remain silent in pain.

Orations, words and politics are rendered off subject before the incomprehensible unknown forces that are compulsively repeated and shake the very foundations of being. We want to know and understand. And all the time we realise that we do not know, we do not understand. We are off. Off subject. The events do not follow a sequence. Time and space are contained and exploded. Episodes of fragmentation and construction happen one after the other.

Apparently, this praise (*egkomion, ἐγκώμιον*) of Athens was received enthusiastically by the ancient audience of *Suppliant Women* (Zuntz, 1955). We can assume that Euripides describes with irony the function of a common omnipotent fantasy of the invincible, beyond catastrophe, in the city of Athens.

Living in the midst of war, after they had suffered a calamity (epidemic), the Athenians must associate with their war dead. They deny and split painful feelings of loss to make them tolerable. They make themselves being and not being present there to live through the experience.

The experience of time changes during wars and epidemics. People die but life does not go on. Life time and space are split in many condensed traumatic experiences and a denied unreal diluted feeling that whatever one struggles for is "off subject", depersonalised, futile, vanished in thin air, impossible to restore.

There is no thought without a subject. Euripides plays with us by oscillating between process and non-process, politics and non-politics, thinking and non-thinking, being and not being a subject. He reminds us that the culture of logos and politics are not to be taken for granted. Beyond reason and words there is a world of supernatural forces and limits of primitive emotional experiences.

The magical flow of time

We know and do not know (we split off) the reality of time intruding in the play, disrupting the sense of immortality and invincibility of individuals and the polis. The reality presented of the wounded bodies, the blood, the flesh and the corpses is so unthinkable, raw, and gruesome that it is met with disbelief.

The critics observe that there is something magical about the flow of time in the *Suppliants*. Before the plot can unexpectedly change course, it ushers in the solution. A climate of harmony is achieved, without conflicts, inside the city that continues to be cohesive. Scully (1995:4) observes that this play offers no point of stability and, once established, leaves no position untested: "This is a masterful work, a dramatic poem of formidable power in its uncompromising juxtapositions of conflicting pulls of human psyche".

Magical fantasies distort the perception of reality and maintain the coherence of the polis. The passage of time, the time of separation, is split off and denied. In 1921, Freud based his idea about the formation of the unity of society on primary identification (imitation) of the infant with the parents. In group situations this primitive early bond is activated. Living an emotional experience is the key to enter areas beyond words and meaning.

Time – flow is streamed by the unconscious movements of affects, which are shaped by the vicissitudes of object relationships (Hartocollis, 1983). As Jaqueline de Romilly (1971) writes, time is examined by Euripides in relationship to human feelings that bring a disorder to his plots. Time is of an emotional order. Talking about time the persons talk about their emotions. There is often impatience and relief, a sense of "at last". The unexpected theatrical act at the last moment saves the situation and makes the passions rise to extreme intensity.

In politics as in drama, along with myths and rituals, a process of imitation unfolds, which resembles infancy where the need to believe is the basis of the sense of the self. We imitate and pretend ourselves to be figures on a stage. Everything "seems" to be like something.

The non-verbal signs give a static sense of time, a manic suspended animation, while the symbol opens the sense of being in the future. In politics as in drama, it all starts like magic, with denials and splittings, a manic suspended animation, and then becomes very real, with pain and guilt, when integration begins. Klein and Winnicott described the depressive position, the outcome of which is the sense of reality and symbol formation. Steiner (2007:257–261) linked these ideas with linguists' theory (Charles Pierce and Roman Jacobson) according to which we create, communicate and complete our experiences with indexes, icons, and verbal symbols that imply each other and are integrated into verbal language.

From unity to transaction with the object

On the way to find-construct reality humans split and project parts of their selves. They create narcissistic doubles, which are similar to them so that reality is not introduced violently and traumatically, and also different from them, so that a first boundary between inside and outside is instituted. A first order is established. An adequate distance allows the otherness of the objects to be perceived, and begin to be internalised.

In order to move from primary to secondary identification, the child invests sameness. This transition involves a transaction between the child and the mother who is similar to the child, a transaction that replaces the feeling of unity with the object. The child (girl or boy) experiences a primary homosexuality (Denis, 1982:643; Parsons, 1990:22; Bell, 2007:7).

The religious ceremonies, the agora, pnyka, theatres, and gymnasia are places where people come together in search of reality. The arrangement of the world by splits of the self is but an aspect of the working of culture (in the rituals, myths, tragedy and politics). Suddenly something new emerges and then another, and another one, always one more, another yet the same. They dramatise the cycles that represent the self and the linear course to the creation-discovery of the object. They have to do with mourning and femininity.

We hope that the dichotomies are flexible – transient states – and capable of being integrated. If they are unbending – permanent structures – and hardened walls that divide, they have an organisation of the world to offer and a contact with reality but they cannot be bridged. Each of their forceful integration causes a traumatic flooding. Politics then fails, being unable to take in the inundating torrents of passion. Confusion prevails as public life is flooded with narcissistic doubles, multiple mirrors of a dead-end dark labyrinth and fears of fragmentation, alternating with paranoid powers. Then the ritualistic sacrifices that target these narcissistic doubles are no more symbolic public feasts but real blood-letting.

Living memories or eternal ghosts?

Euripides offers two medicines for pain. Time heals the pain and passions do not last forever. However, time and forgetting are ineffective consolations. The lasting medicine that conquers pain and death is memory.

The play and the public life which it mirrors are filled with struggles of contradictory experiences that are compulsively repeated. The initiated internalisation processes bring these struggles to a conclusion by negotiation. The conclusion comes when lasting, binding memories are inscribed ineffably.

Theseus is given the power to lead and find out who he and his polis truly are. He is placed before contradictory elements, which lie beyond the order of politics. He undertakes to give meaning and integrate these untranslated elements in a way that keeps the unity of his city. These are "enigmas" (impossible links according to Aristotle's Poetics, cited by Arvanitakis, 1998:958).

One thing that the leader is afraid of is not being able to test reality. Reality is unavoidable. Politics is the art of the attainable and the possible. The impossible thing is omnipotence, which makes the leader ignorant of reality. At certain moments there are "no alternatives within an action" (Williams, 1993:146).

Throughout the agon, Theseus and the Herald try not to settle an issue but to establish "the bounds of opposition that will brook no compromise" (Burian, 1985:140). The *Suppliants* reshapes an Attic myth in order for the community to be immersed in the common pool of imagination. The poet absorbs the myriad unintelligible elements and recreates, using the canvas of a myth, a comprehensive image.

A polis is always in crisis. In periods of transition the polis struggles to re-invent its identity. The open-ended outcome leaves many threads of meaning that are available for us to pick. The rhythms of the polis are disturbed inside us. There is no way to predict at the beginning the outcome of the process of transformations. Only during the crisis and afterwards do we struggle to understand.

The play is full of contemplations on an undemanding playful celebration of peace and life, the integrity of a democratic polis sustained by the rule of law, necessity for war, and the position of the gods. Does man have the free will to act? Is hubris inherent in human nature (Kovacs, 1998)?

How does one become a subject of his polis? How are the links of holding together the city forged? Where do those who die in war go? Are they placed where they belong, in the past, as our living memories? Are they eternal undead ghosts appearing in incomprehensible displays of demonic enactments within the polis?

The gravity of the myth

We do not need to relate the tragedy to any historical era. Tragedy makes history out of the experiences of the personal and collective past, which it dramatises and interprets on stage. It gives the world order, pace, rhythm, psychic and civic ethos. "Suppliant Women conjoins mythical Athens with its living counterpart. . . . (I)t demonstrates that tragic myths possessed sufficient gravity to hold the contemporary world within their orbit, creating a wide spatial field in which mythic and contemporary worlds could coexist" (Rhem, 2002:30).

A myth contains in its core grains of historical truth that gives the story a sense of conviction. Freud (1901:259) believes that the construction of supernatural reality mirrors the obscure recognition of unconscious processes. Freud (1912–13:93) writes:

> If the survivors' position in relation to the dead was really what first caused primitive man to reflect, and compelled him to hand over some of his omnipotence to the spirits and to sacrifice some of his freedom of action, then these cultural products would constitute a first acknowledgment of Ανάγκη, [Necessity], which opposes human narcissism.

Gods and humans alike obey Necessity (*Anagke, Ἀνάγκη*). The chorus of Euripides' Alkestis sings the hymn to the goddess of Necessity [978–979]: "For whatever Zeus decides only with your consent he makes it happen".

A myth is a witness of prehistory. It is an invention that constructs an answer to the question of peoples' origins. Myths contain the grain of historical truth, a weight, a centre of gravity, a portion of the traumatic perception that escaped representation and which can be re-constructed afterwards (Freud, 1916–17:391, 1920, 1937b:267–269).

The tragic poet reshapes the myth to reflect realities of politics so that they can be recognised and rendered metaphorically on stage. Politics resembles a play; it stands in between the audience and the poet (Winnicott, 1971:100). The tragic plot helps us bear the meaning that makes our reality real.

A tragedy is part of its time and is also relevant today. Its codes help us interpret the experiences we share with others today. Tragedy, like history, is both research and a quest. It is an open-ended process that allows us to know, that is, to transform reality. When at the end of the *Suppliants* the sons of the Seven carry the bones of their fathers and vow to avenge their deaths, the ancient audience must have associated them with the war orphans, present in the front seats of the theatre.

In 5th century Athens, before the greater Dionysia, every March, an impressive festive procession brings Dionysus' statue from outside the city to the theatre. Dithyrambs are sung in honour of the god, wine flows freely and huge phalli are carried through the streets. On the next day, the war orphans' parade takes place in the streets of Athens honouring their fathers who died defending the city. They then take the front seats in the theatre. Only then the play begins. "The evocation of this presentation of the orphans in the theatre is a topos of political rhetoric" (Loraux, 2002:17–18). One of the play's political functions is to prevent the people from feeling devoid of meaning, like being in a desert, wandering as orphans of meaning.

The speaking-acting subject

Myths contain grains of reality – in constant need of meaning – which makes them immortal. Through drama, Athens interprets its prehistoric myths with words and actions, transforming them into a tragic plot. A myth "documents" – envelops with meaning the story of – a shared reality that is repeated beyond time and resists mourning. Tragedy inserts in this mythic narration the chronicle of a tragic plot that is realised within time and space.

Through drama Athens also enters the myths of other cities (Storey, 2008:13): Theseus enters the myth of the Seven who were killed at Thebes.

The *Suppliants* converges on the myth of the lethal battle between Oedipus' children.

We can think that public life is realised through words and actions. Theatre is the art of politics par excellence. The speaking-acting subject presents his self publicly with meaningful statements. Drama (from the verb "thran", δρᾶν, which means "acting") is part of politics (Arendt, 1958:188).

By reflecting our experiences, the poet makes them suitable for integration in public life; he reshapes them into material from which community links will be forged. Public life originates in the act of expression. It is based on the unconscious movement of repetitious retracing and enacting of represented and unrepresented experiences on the stage of one's consciousness and those of the others, in the language of words and deeds, and of the body (Scarfone, 2011:82).

Through the tragic plot, shared ghosts come to life out of their semi-existence, appearing at a specific place and time. Drama stages sequences of actions and words, gives the ghosts reality and convincing historical truth, an outcome of mourning through reconciliation and memory.

Athens is not an inactive city that works clandestinely and warily. Athens is an active city whose meddlesomeness (*polypragmosyne, πολυπραγμοσύνη*) brings its citizens many labours and rewards. Throughout the play women and men speak on their acts and act on their words, proudly proving that their city cannot rest and cannot leave other cities at rest. Labour, (*ponos, πόνος*), is a key word in the play.

Storey (2008:51) writes:

> Thucydides (1.70) has an envoy from Corinth to Sparta argue how inaction is foreign to the Athenian character and how their success owes much to action rather than to caution: "for they are innovators (*neôteropoioi*), quick to formulate plans and to put into practice whatever they decide . . . in all this they toil with labours (*ponoi*) and dangers all the days of their lives . . . and they consider an uninvolved and peaceful life (*hêsychian apragmona*) as much of a misfortune and active life (*ascholian epiponon*)".

The order (kosmos, κόσμος) of intellect and of passion (pathos, πάθος)

Burian (1985:130–132) observes: The play offers two contrasting "orderings of reality. . . . The first . . . the *kosmos* (*κόσμος*) of emotion . . . embodied chiefly in the suppliant women . . .; the second *kosmos* that of intellect is represented above all by Theseus". The play begins with the *kosmos* of emotion, the deep sorrow of the lamenting mothers. . . . Theseus (represents) . . . the *kosmos* of intellect. Men need to look inside themselves to see that they are responsible for their experiences. The gods have brought man out of bestial confusion through the gift of prudence (*sunesis, σύνεσις*) and its interpreter, language (*glossa, γλῶσσα*). "The gods even guide men, when intelligence is insufficient, by prophecy and sacrificial divination. Adrastos . . . assumed that he understood the oracle and used it to justify what no wise man would attempt, the mating of justice to injustice".

The stage philosopher is also a prophet. He is a poet who uses both logos and pathos that reach truths beyond meaning.

> First, he granted us reason, and then tongue
> As messenger of words, to enable speech.
> . . .
> As for the mysteries and things we don't clearly know,
> our priests read them in fore and pry in the folds
> of entrails and decipher birds in flight

[204–214]

Burian (1985:133–140) describes brilliantly the oscillation between reason and passion in politics: Theseus' debate with Adrastos, his first "political analysis", demonstrates that humans are responsible for their actions. They should "not mingle . . . foul with fair, unjust with just". The leader has doubts about accepting the suit of his suppliants "but it is out of the question that he finally rejects it". Adrastos orders the grieving women to get ready to depart leaving the branches at the altar around Aithra and calling on Demeter and all gods to be witnesses to the rejection of their supplications by Theseus. "Even a beast (*thēr, θήρ*) has a cave for refuge, they say". The metaphor of beast brings many associations of untamed wild forces of passion.

Theseus initially treats misfortune as a problem of judgment, and he overlooks the human suffering. Aithra's tears cause Theseus distress but also give her a chance to link religious, political, civil, and personal considerations in a complex chain. Her tears are transformed into an argument. She decides not to remain silent because of the injustice that was done to the Suppliants (Burian, 1985:141–142).

Aithra's political speech enables Theseus to bridge contradictory aspects of public life and turn them into paradoxes. Then he can feel a receptive visceral sympathy towards the mothers' pain on a deep psychosomatic level. The ethics of sympathy, friendship and pity, contain the Suppliants. The indwelling of humans and wild animals is called "ethos" even since Homer's time. It is unthinkable for man to wander off limits without being bound by a human canon, without being linked to an object. The rule of law provides this refuge of containment for man.

The rulers have the right to decide but the rule of law in a democratic polis prevents them from abusing this power. The excessive ambition and lack of links of friendship and pity towards others is hubris. Moderation is needed in democracy.

How much of a shock can a bridge bear?

Politics is an answer to the question of how much reality can a polis bear? How much meaning and truth can it struggle with? How much meaningless-ness can it tolerate? Politics is the process of making a decision about how much shock the bridge can sustain when action is taken to cross the borders and transgress the lines of the unknown.

People set out on a course (*poreia, πορεία*) in order to fill the gaps *(apo-ria, απορία)* of time and space, the disruptions, of their selves and the polis, making them coherent. A point is inevitably reached where no words and ideas can contain the madness of passions. When politics fails to construct adequate links of meaning, then men and women sacrifice and literally offer their bodies as bridges to fill the gap of irreducible splits. They fall in the chasms of society and they are lost.

Agonies of annihilation, anxieties about boundaries and fears of being attacked from the outside happen in moments of transition to integra-tion (Winnicott, 1974:105, 1988:121, 124). We can think that something analogous happens in a polis. Facing a new integration, Theseus reacts by attacking Adrastos' supplication as a threat to the coherence of his city.

Aithra offers a different kind of defence to the coherence of the polis' social fabric. The city needs men with political responsibility, not silent ones. It is held together by those who preserve the human and divine laws. In suppliant dramas the protector is forced to wage war on the suppliants' behalf.

The dramatic relevance of Aithra's argument lies in her linking political considerations with religious, ethical and personal arguments that call for action. This deep feminine intelligence contains the seed of the tragic, the emergence of an autonomous subject from a primary union. The emerging individual keeps from the state of the union a basic element. This is the feminine capacity of being receptive and passive towards an experience to which he becomes subject.

Greeks love to wrestle and argue in gymnasia and in the agora. The political play of *Suppliant Women* could not but be full of arguments (Zuntz, 1955:6). In a debate each participant returns to the other what he throws away. The feminine is what all men and women repudiate. From the beginning of the play there is an oscillation of focus between the role of the chorus – public voice of women performing religious or mourning rites – and the speeches and actions about politics.

Something in the depth of public life is kept mute. Out of fear of breaking down the bridges and the unthinkable anxiety of falling into the abyss and "falling off" the world, people keep quiet and hold their breath. However, they suddenly speak and take a breath of life; they are born subjects of their thoughts.

Humans need to be free to play within bounds. This is possible in the theatre. We can think of the open mouth of the Greek theatrical mask as symbolising both the speechlessness of the terrified person and "tragedy's need to bear spoken witness to the unspeakable, to keep talking in the face of horror" (Rhem, 2002:7).

The grieving mothers speak out and make their pain a public affair. Aithra will not stay silent. She will not hide her thoughts and feelings.

> . . . Nor should fear
> make me veil what I know to be right

[296–297]

Aithra opens the space for women to speak and Athena closes the play with her decisive intervention, instructing men to endow their words with the reality of action. Theseus and the Herald deliver political speeches to find out that there are areas which lie beyond words and meaning.

A completed experience

Nothing can be completed until it passes through speech [113], says Euripides at the beginning of the play. Logos constructs a meaning that gives coherence to the plot. However, Theseus first verbal reaction to Adrastos is incomplete. The key words here are the completion of an experience. An experience should be complete before one can learn from it. Only when the object survives one's ruthless attacks of the drives and becomes external enough, outside the area of his omnipotence, does one become a subject of the experience.

Theseus invites Adrastos to give a funeral oration for the dead for the sake of educating (*paideia, παιδεία*) young people. The idea is that the funeral oration would complete the experience. This is a chance to share experiences and learn from them with the citizens getting involved and forming links of identity among themselves.

The *Suppliants* is a lesson about friendship and pity as basic ingredients of public life in a democracy. Theseus introduces politics when he asks Adrastos to deliver a funeral oration.

THESEUS: But I won't make a joke of it by demanding
A blow by blow account, who stood against whom
In battle, and the spear wounds each received.
That's idle chatter, for listener and teller both,
And nonsense to think a man plunged in fighting
with a hail of spears before his eyes, could see
clearly enough to tell who's heroic.

[805–811]

Adrastos' speech changes the mood from lyric grief to public praise. He feels obliged, "not unwillingly" [817], to find something idealising to say, which will inspire the young and set up his dead friends as examples of personal and civic virtue.

The critics observe the irony of the funeral orations between the actual deeds of the deceased and the clichés that are uttered, on the one hand, and personal pain and public need on the other. The villains of the myth are presented as fighting men who commit themselves to civil values.

Storey (2008:68) writes: "These young men whose desire and clamour for war has ruined themselves, their families, and their citizens, are ironically presented as champions of the very institutions that they ruined". The poet's theatrical ingenuity enables us to see that we go back and forth between a heroic and an ironic view of the world, between positive and negative aspects of the truth we construct. In this play full of irony and tension, Euripides reminds us that history is written by those who narrate it, not by those who live it, and the victor's version of it prevails over that of the vanquished. Adrastos praises his friends whom he led to death. He tells a truth through a funeral speech, which is familiar to Athenians.

Perikles's Funeral Oration (*Epitaph, Ἐπιτάφιος*) was given to us by "the fourth tragic poet", Thucydides as a founding text of democracy. It is the epitome of the mourning process (Thucydides', 1910). Loraux (1986) pointed out that the epitaph was an institution of Athenian Democracy, a praise (*epainos, ἔπαινος*) to the city, which celebrated the Athenian citizen and invented a complex image of Athens. It praised the "fine" death of the citizen in battle, a noble aristocratic ethos. It also fostered the superiority of collective and public action as opposed to the private and individual one.

The old King adds a lesson of deep ironic significance. "Even an infant learns to speak and hear the things he does not know. So, train children well". Irony does not lie in the courage of men who bravely died in an insane war that brought disaster to all. We are soon to see the pattern of these men's lives emerge in their sons. What the Epigonoi "learn" from their fathers' lives (and deaths) shows the failure of reasoned discourse, the foundation of Theseus' optimistic *kosmos*, to change this pattern (Burian, 1985:148–149).

We can surmise that what Euripides is trying to show is how two contradictory views are allowed by politics to coexist as a paradox in the public life of a moderate democracy. Each one has its place in a transitional space of poetry, religion, and politics alike.

On the one hand, Euripides questions idealisations and is subversive to the establishment. On the other hand, he maintains the values of civil life. Politics preserves the situation in which people can make freely and securely a move towards separation, mourning, integration, and autonomy, while at the same time it keeps alive the fear of "parental" authority in the rule of law, which protects them from being omnipotent and therefore on the verge of collapse. Every "completion" in the process of politics is in reality incomplete. An episode may be terminated but the process never ends. A new question always arises.

The final lesson on objectivity in the domain of politics is given to Theseus by goddess Athena herself. Politics is possible, as an effort – to create a common ground of reality – outside the fantasy of omnipotence. The democratic polis holds – gives time to – a shared experience long enough for it to be completed and integrated. Learning from experience takes place on the prototype of a mother holding her infant, which emerges as a separate subject capable of thinking, acting, and speaking.

The narcissistic contract

The dead are given their place. The children take the place of the dead. Aulagnier (1975) developed her idea of narcissistic contract, based on Freud's (1914) introduction to narcissism and Castoriadis' (1975) studies on the processes in which children become the subjects of their social group: A child is born in an oedipal space, the bounds of which are innately structured and also realised in his family by his two parents and himself.

Freud (1940a:149) examined how the influences of the past generations and the contemporary culture are transmitted though the parents' to the child's superego. The parental influence "of course includes in its operations not only the personalities of the actual parents but also the family, racial, and national traditions handed on through them, as well was the demands of the immediate social *milieu* which they represent".

The parental couple's relationship with the culture transmits to the child the law of the social group with which they share common ideals. Through the parents, the social group invests the child and prepares a space in the society for it. In this place the child is expected to stand as a subject of the collective fantasies of the group, to become a future voice, speak on behalf of the dead and repeat statements of those whose place it has come to occupy. This transmission guarantees that the child will have his own independent place in a continuous cycle of rebirth and regeneration of the body.

The child internalises a primary illusion of an atemporal immortal existence of the self, which he projects onto his social group. In this way he believes that the polis is an invincible body that never dies. The child forms an ego ideal, part of his superego, which is shaped by the superego of his parents, which in turn is inherited from the previous generations and shaped by the current socio-cultural ideologies of the social institutions. The parents' unfulfilled narcissistic aspirations are transmitted to the child. The child becomes a subject in their mirroring eyes and in those of their polis. The ego ideal is a projection of the child's narcissism onto his parents, whose responses provide a projected future integration and contribute to the formation of the ego ideal. The growing child feels that he carries the burden forward and holds the world in his hands. If the child's ideal is not validated, then the law is also invalid and the destruction of the polis itself is imminent.

Following Aulagnier's theory and attending Euripides' play, we may assume that the social group is formed by alliances of individual voices sharing the same language and making the same mythical, mystical, religious, poetic, philosophical, and scientific statements. These alliances contain the individuals' struggles to transform reality.

Kaës (2007) has helped us think about the community alliances we form. The question is how to be true to oneself, autonomous, and at the same time a subject of his social group. The way the others interpret the experiences and the fantasies one projects to them does not only explain but also shape one as subject to them.

Inherent in the forming of alliances in the community is violence. Violence is inherent in institutions. It originates in omnipotent fantasies that distort the experiences of reality, which the individuals recreate with their social group, and cease to be speaking and acting subjects. They become silent, hidden in areas of deprivation of meaning and deficit of identity.

The capacity to be a tragic subject

What are we left with after the emergence from the primary union and the shock from the loss of omnipotence? We are left with the capacity to struggle. This is a life-long struggle to differentiate and link the internal with the external reality in the third transitional reality. The subject enters the space of transitional phenomena in order to face the immense shock of the loss of omnipotence (Winnicott, 1971:71).

Euripides' *Suppliants* presents the crushing of Argos on account of hubris (failed to be a functional state) and Thebes (ruled by a despotic, arrogant ruler). Is Athens close to hubris too? The Messenger's reference to arrogant people – who are unable to wait and are escalating a situation – may be "a poignant commentary on the tragedy of Athenian politics" (Storey, 2008:57).

We can think of hubris as a defence of arrogance against the agony of disintegration that is felt when a step toward a new integration (internalisation) is taken. This step toward integration makes one a tragic subject. Hubris and the crushing of omnipotence constitute the core of ancient tragedy. They depict the tragic position that the infant painfully attains when he breaks from the illusion of a primary union and emerges as an individual entity.

The movement from non-integration to integration, which brings the threat of disintegration, requires the organising of impulses, defences, affects, and ego functions into the taking of a position. This is a tragic position.

Arvanitakis (1998) relied on Euripides's Bacchae and Aristotle's interpretation in order to examine the essence of the tragic. The defining moment of the tragic is the pathos of fragmentation, as its Dionysiac origin points out. There is a mutative movement from the myth of an original unity to the logos of differentiation, which represents a formative violent act in the service of the drives of Eros. Logos aims at constructing a meaning that integrates contradictions and gives coherence to the plot.

O Freud (1937a, 1937b, 1940b) in his responsive texts to Ferenczi (1933) identified splitting. The subject is not a given. Now we can think that before anything happens in human development, the infant needs to attain the "tragic position", the status of being a separate entity, after the first stable integration of his ego.

The separation from the primary union results in the loss of omnipotence, which is a shock for the emerging infant. The environment mother holds the infant in the beginning of his life when it has absolute need of her care. Because of its mother's adequate adaptation to its ego needs, the infant can know nothing of its dependence, nothing of the external reality and nothing of its existence. In separating from the primary union, the child emerges as an integrated subject. It emerges as a subject of (internalises) its drives of love and hate, its male and female elements and its omnipotence (Winnicott, 1960:44, 1963:74–75, 1971).

The mother fosters in her psychic space the experiences that the infant imparts on her (she temporarily becomes another subject for them). She metabolises and reflects them back to it. The infant internalises its metabolised experiences and the way they are processed by its mother. In this way it creates a space of its own where it can internalise the experiences of which it becomes the subject (Freud, 1915:126–129).

In order for the infant to create a psychic space with a boundary to the outside, the mother must first make room inside her to accommodate this. A newborn has before anything else the experience of its mother taking it inside her, introjecting it. The infant then introjects its introjecting mother and creates inside it a psychic space of its own where it can receive the new experiences (Bick, 1968:484–485).

Aisenstein (2019) remarked: Psychic functioning should not be confused with thinking. Thoughts require a subject who thinks of them and an internal object that returns the confirmation of investment to it, as Green has observed (1991). In his work on Negation, Freud (1925) described the original "no" of the child that separates inside from outside, and becomes the origin of the subject. By contrast, the splitting of the ego is a rift that never heals (Freud (1940b). It signals the non-dialectical co-existence of an affirmation and a negation.

Aisenstein (2017:205) wrote: Thinking is an "act of the flesh" and the mysterious leaps form mind to body are marked with acts, violence, pain, somatisations and destructions of thought processes. It exists not only in pathological organisations but also in a more general way. "That is my hypothesis. I see the early splittings of the ego as organising the denials which underlie submission to authority, the loss of the capacity to think in terms of 'I', in short, a conformist dementalization".

The child emerging from the symbiosis becomes a tragic subject. The loss of omnipotence in tragedy represents the downfall on account of hubris after which things begin to happen. The things that begin to happen are all those ordeals that the subject has to go through in order to put in a safe place the meaning he makes and internalises. He needs a safe place to keep his meaning and the emerging self.

The subject struggles to emerge, separate from, and preserve the substratum of the legitimate illusion that safeguards his narcissistic integrity. He then becomes a subject of his polis, which supports his ego ideal. He begins to live inside space and time; he experiences conflicts and traumas, transformations and impasses, losses, ruptures, and splits that occur in psychic and social topography and history.

Doomed to an imperfect society

A child moves from the relationship with his mother to the one with his father and then to the parental couple. From there he steps outside the bounds of the family to enter his social group. At each step he renounces the certainties he had before. The child puts on the yoke of the necessity to be born a subject of – to internalise – the supernatural forces that planned his birth long before. The child is harnessed to the need of realising with his two parents the innate triangular structure, to live, and internalise the oedipal situation.

Euripides presents the conflict between generations. The play introduces a new leader with a new spear in a new version of the story. Adrastos was accused by the young leader of Athens of having been led astray by the hot-headed youths (*neoi, νέοι*) who clamour for glory and pursue unjust and destructive wars. The shouting of the young men confounded the old King. The young are revolutionary (*neoterizein, νεωτερίζειν*) and the new is ominous (Storey, 2008:32–37, 64).

The plot of the Suppliants is tragic. It shows the struggle of the subjects to constitute an oedipal situation. The play does not end until the sons of the dead assume the guilt as responsible subjects of their fathers' deaths. No father can die until he finds someone to murder him and take his place. No one can die until a body is retrieved and identified. No one's remains can be buried until the subject guilty of the murder comes forward to assume responsibility.

Burian (1985:155) concludes:

> Those who have tried to understand the play as patriotic drama, and equally those who have seen in it a thoroughgoing satirical or ironic intent, seem to expect it to preach its truth. It withholds that comfort, insisting that even admirable aspirations and achievements are beset by uncertainty and subject to distortion by passion and the passage of time. Its complex structure corresponds to a complex vision. The Suppliant Women . . . is nevertheless political to the very core, a tragedy of men and women doomed not to heroic isolation, but to an imperfect society, for better or worse.

References

Aisenstein M. (2017) *An Analytic Journey: From the Art of Archery to the Art of Psychoanalysis*. London, Karnac.

———. (2019) *Desir-Douleur-Pensee*. In Greek (Trans. S. Leonidi, Ed. P. Aloupis). Athens, Agra Publications.

Arendt H. (1958) *The Human Condition*. Chicago, Chicago University Press.

Aristotle's. (1996) *Poetics*. (Trans. Malcom Hearth). New York, Penguin Books.

Arvanitakis K. (1998) Some Thoughts on the Essence of the Tragic. *International Journal of Psycho-Analysis*, *79*(5), 955–964.

Aulagnier P. (1975 [2001]) *The Violence of Interpretation: From Pictogram to Statement*. London and New York, Routledge.

Bell D. (2007) Psychoanalytic Perspectives on the Dionysiac and the Apollonian in Euripides's Bacchae. In C. Bainbridge, et al. (Eds.) *Culture and the Unconscious*. Basingstoke UK, Palgrave MacMillan.

Bick E. (1968) The Experience of the Skin in Early Object-Relations. *International Journal of Psycho-Analysis*, *49*, 484–486.

Burian P. (1985) Logos and Pathos: The Politics of the Suppliant Women. In P. Burian (Ed.) *Directions in Euripidean Criticism: A Collection of Essays*. Durham, NC, Duke University Press.

Castoriadis C. (1975) *L'Institution imaginaire de la société*. Paris, Seuil. In Greek (Trans. S. Halikias, G. Spantidaki and K. Spantidakis, Ed. K. Spantidakis). Athens, Kedros (1981).

Denis P. (1982) Primary Homosexuality: A Foundation of Contradictions. In D. Briksted-Breen, S. Flandres and A. Gibeault (Eds.) *Reading French Psychoanalysis*. London and New York, Routledge (2010).

De Romilly J. (1971) *Le Temps dans la Tragedie Grecque*. Paris, VRIN.

Euripides'. (1995) *Suppliant Women*. (Trans. R. Warren and S. Scully). Oxford, Oxford University Press.

Ferenczi S. (1933 [1955]) The Confusion of Tongues between Adults and the Child:. The Language of Tenderness and of Passion. In *Final Contributions to the Problems and Methods of Psychoanalysis*. (Trans. E. Mosbacher, et al.). London, Maresfield Reprints.

Freud S. (1901) The Psychology of Everyday Life. *S.E., 6.*

———. (1912–1913) Totem and Taboo: Some Points of Agreement between the Mental Lives of Savages and Neurotics. *S.E., 13.*

———. (1914) On Narcissism: An Introduction. *S.E., 14.*

———. (1915) Instincts and Their Vicissitudes. *S.E., 14.*

———. (1916–1917) Introductory Lectures on Psycho-Analysis. *S.E., 14.*

———. (1920) Beyond the Pleasure Principle. *S.E., 18.*

———. (1921) Group Psychology and the Analysis of the Ego. *S.E., 18.*

———. (1925) Negation. *S.E., 19.*

———. (1937a) Analysis Terminable and Interminable. *S.E., 23.*

———. (1937b) Constructions in Analysis. *S.E., 23.*

———. (1940a) An Outline of Psychoanalysis. *S.E., 23.*

———. (1940b) Splitting of the Ego in the Process of Defence. *S.E., 23.*

Green A. (1980) Thésée et Oedipe. Une iterprétation psychanalytique de la Théséide. In *Psychanalyse et Culture Greque. Confluents Psychanalytique*. Paris, Les Belles Lettres. In Greek (Trans. M. Fragopoulos). Athens, Rappa (1985).

———. (1991 [2001]) *Narcissism de vie, narcissism de mort*. Paris, Minuit. English trans. *Life Narcissism, Death Narcissism*. (Trans. A. Weller). London, Free Association Books.

Grube G. (1941) *The Drama of Euripides*. London, Methuen.

Hartocollis P. (1983) *Time and Timelessness*. New York, International Universities Press.

Kaës R. (2007) *Linking, Alliances and Shared Space: Groups and the Psychoanalyst*. London, The International Psychoanalytic Library.

Kitto H. (1961) *Greek Tragedy*. London and New York, Routledge.

Knox B. (1985) Euripides: The Poet as Prophet. In P. Burian (Ed.) *Directions in Euripidean Criticism: A Collection of Essays*. Durham, Duke University Press.

Kovacs D. (1998) *Euripides: Suppliant Women, Electra, Heracles*. Cambridge, MA, Harvard University Press.

Loraux N. (1986) *The Invention of Athens: The Funeral Oration in the Classical City*. Cambridge, MA, Harvard University Press.

———. (2002) *The Mourning Voice: An Essay on Greek Tragedy*. London, Cornell University Press.

Parsons M. (1990) Self-Knowledge Refused and Accepted. *Journal of Analytic Psychology*, *35*(1), 19–40.

Rhem R. (1992) *Greek Tragic Theatre*. London and New York, Routledge.

———. (2002) *The Play of Space: Spatial Transformation in Greek Tragedy*. Princeton and Oxford, Princeton Universities Press.

Scarfone D. (2011) Repetition: Between Presence and Meaning. *Canadian Journal of Psychoanalysis*, *19*(1), 70–86.

Scully S. (1995) Introduction. In *Euripides, Suppliant Women* (Trans. Rosanna Warren and Stephen Scully). Oxford, Oxford University Press.

Steiner R. (2007) Does the Pierce's Semiotic Model Based on Index, Icon, Symbol Have Anything to Do with Psychoanalysis? In G. Ambrosio, S. Argentieri and J. Canestri (Eds.) *Language, Symboliszation, and Psychosis: Essays in Honour of Jacqueline Amati Mehler*. London, Karnac.

Storey C. (2008) *Euripides: Suppliant Women*. London, Duckworth.

Thucydides'. (1910) *The Peloponnesian War*. London, J. M. Dent; New York, E. P. Dutton.

Williams B. (1993) *Shame and Necessity*. Berkeley and Los Angeles, University of California Press.

Winnicott D. (1960 [1990]) The Theory of Parent-Infant Relationship. In *The Maturational Processes and the Facilitating Environment*. London, Karnac Books.

———. (1963 [1990]) The Development of the Capacity for Concern. In *The Maturational Processes and the Facilitating Environment*. London, Karnac Books.

———. (1971) *Playing and Reality*. London, Tavistock.

———. (1974) The Fear of Breakdown. *International Review of Psychoanalysis*, *1*, 103–107.

———. (1988) *Human Nature*. London, Free Association Books.

Zuntz G. (1955) *The Political Plays of Euripides*. Manchester, Manchester University Press.

3 The work of mourning

Sotiris Manolopoulos

The polis has rules on how and where to express publicly the personal pain of grieving. The state, through the politics of lamentation, regulates the rituals because the savage emotions of mourning may become dangerous to the political order. Unresolved mourning can be the source of future political conflicts, even wars.

Storey (2008:79) reminds us that Solon's laws restricted the intense public expression of mourning. Perikles instructed the women of Athens not to indulge in grief too much (Thucydides, 2.445).

Loraux (2002:14–26) observed that the Athenians had reorganised the space at the beginning of the 5th century BC and separated the agora and the assembly from the theatre. The issues that the citizens of Athens preferred to ignore came back in the civic space of the tragic theatre. The theatre was an Athenian institution, political, civic, and democratic. Theatre and assembly contributed to the political function of public speech. The agora was for politics, where reason without emotion was needed. In this sense the city was an anti-tragic machine. The theatre was a place for the expression of passions; it was an anti-political institution. It threatened the defences that maintained the ideology of the city; it brought to light the contradictions inherent in the nature of politics.

The *Suppliants* bring the theatre into the agora. Its tragic effect is closely related to the work of mourning that helps the city recognise that there are limits to its omnipotence and allows the integration processes. This recognition makes democracy a tragic regime.

The *Suppliants* is divided in two parts. In the first, the mothers' supplication has led to war and the retrieval of the dead. The first part concerns the political supplication and the response to it with a war in defence of the law. The second part concerns the recognition of the mere reality of the first, what is called the first death, the physical one, and the initiation of the second death, the psychological one.

DOI: 10.4324/9781003252184-4

In the second part of the play, the rituals of mourning are re-enacted and changes of mood are sudden and sharp while the meaning of words shifts abruptly (Scully, 1995). The pathos of the scene reaches a poignant depth when the bodies of the dead are brought on stage in sight of their mothers but beyond their reach. The dead are there on the stage, absolutely separate, alone, inaccessible, a source of pernicious agony and lethal guilt.

Rescuing the dead

When the Messenger enters with news from the battlefield the mothers ask:

CHORUS: What news do you bring?
How will Athena's army stand the test?
Did you speak with spears? Or word to word?
May victory come! But if Ares preferred
death, if the city fills with groans,
with gashes, blood, and beaten beasts,
what word, what accusation will be heard?

[580–586]

Accusations? The mourners idealise the dead and project their aggression (against the dead) on others, who are then felt as if accusing them with unjust criticisms. In order for the dead to be restored, after the physical death, a second one, is accomplished psychically in public rituals. The mourning is a public affair.

In response to the news of Theseus' victory, the tone of Adrastos' speech is despairing.

> Adrastos' speech forms a bridge between the two main parts of the play. The recovery of the fallen warriors has been accomplished; what follows is . . . a series of startling and disturbing scenes, linked by the presence of the longed for dead (that) constitutes a second action which, like the first, will move from the personal to the political, and from sentiments to deeds.
>
> (Burian, 1985:145)

This was a campaign to "rescue" the dead. This meant giving them their second, proper death. If the dead are not properly buried, they will have a wretched death. They will not be honoured or spoken of by the living with words that keep their memory and fame alive. The Messenger informs us that Theseus has undertaken the labour to wash the bodies of the war dead with his own hands and prepare them for cremation. He does the same for the common soldiers. He buries them separately, near the rock of Eleutherai on Mount Cithairon. This is a burden undertaken by women or slaves. Reason is a slave to passion. It is a terrible burden but it is not shame, it is an act of courage to suffer our passions.

ADRASTOS: What a terrible burden and shame to take on himself!
MESSENGER: Why should we think of our common griefs as shame?
ADRASTOS: Oh gods- I wish I had died with them.
MESSENGER: Your laments are useless. You're making the women weep.
ADRASTOS: Yes. They are my teachers now.
But I'll go and raise my hands to greet the dead
and pour out the hymns of death for my friends
who have left me in my misery to weep
alone. This is the only mortal loss
whose expense can't be recovered: the mortal soul.
Lost money can be restored, not human life.

[730–740]

Proper death cannot happen without the corpse of the dead being identified, buried, and mourned. It cannot happen if no subject is found to take the guilt for their death. The corpses of the Seven are brought on stage. Their sight is an undeniable proof of the loss. When the bodies of the dead are retrieved, the mothers lose the objects of their desperate search and are left with their irretrievable loss. Then, an unending woe begins.

The tragic plot inserts time and subject into the myth. It completes a process of symbolisation that introduces the element of future. Only when something has an end does it last. An end brings changes, and the other. The Greek words for change (*allage, ἀλλαγή*) and other (*allos, ἄλλος*) have the same etymological root. The verb "to change" (*allasso, ἀλλάσσω*) also means "to take revenge" as Orestes said when he arrived in secret at the land of Argos after having received the god's oracle that he should murder his father's murderers.[1]

By contrast to modern avengers, who gird on the explosives and blow themselves and the world to pieces, Orestes had a tragic poet to tell his story. Aeschylus placed him in a tragic plot to suffer his passions and yoke the necessity to integrate his split off elements, becoming a tragic subject. The outcome of *The Eumenides* (*Εὐμενίδες*), the final play of Aeschylus' *Oresteia*, was the integration of primitive elements and the development of social order. Orestes was hunted down and tormented by the Furies (*Erinues, Ἐρινύες*) and found refuge in Athens. He pleaded to Athena who set up a trial in Areopagus (the Hill of Ares) the location of a court that was comprised by twelve citizens, and presided by the goddess herself. Athena casted the decisive vote and Orestes was released (*ap-allasso, ἀπ-αλλάσσω*). After the trial the Furies felt dishonoured by the younger gods and threatened to fling upon the earth the drops of venom that could cause the leafless blight. Athena used persuasion. With gracious words and persistence, she convinced them to give their blessings, and in ex-change (*ant-allasso, ἀντ-αλλάσσω*) she offered them to co-habit along with her polis. The Furies became Eumenides (the gracious ones) and they were given a place in Athens, since not only the confidence to the institutions, but also fear is necessary for people to be persuaded to keep social order.

In Euripides' *Suppliant Women*, Aithra made an ethical choice and used maternal persuasion to support it publicly. Foley (2001) showed how the tragic poetry uses gender relations to speak about crucial issues in the life of the polis. Tragic mothers in Euripides' plays make important contributions in politics.

Death to death

In Euripides' *Suppliants*, the chorus of the mothers is split between fear and confidence.

A: Useless mothers of useless generals-
What green terror lodges in my entrails?

[578–579]

B: Thebes' luck may turn this time, and wrench her fire:
this hope binds courage all around my fear.
A: You speak of the spirits of justice.
B: What others give fortune to us?
A: The gods give many things to bear.
B: You are done by an old fear.
Justice called to justice, death to death.
The gods, who know everything on earth
Will end, grant ease to mortal care.

[587–595]

The mothers sing to the dead. The blood of the fallen answers them confirming their commitment to revenge, to a new cycle of bloodshed.

CHORUS: But for me to look on my son's
corpse, is horror and beauty –
longed for, unhoped – for day

seen at last greatest in fears.
Time, the ancient father
of days, should have let me stay
unmarried forever here
Why should I need sons?

[746–752]

The Suppliants' singing "always" (*aei, ἀεί*) belongs to all-powerful Time, the "ancient father" (*palaios pater, παλαιός πατήρ*). The sense of "always" for mortals is the perpetual repetition of the interruption of temporality in the recurrence of life's vicissitudes. The mourning mothers sing in desperation and their songs, mixed with tears, resonate with the promise that they will mourn forever and their attachment to their tears will be unbreakable (Loraux, 2002:30, 35). The Epigonoi will take revenge; for the sake of the fathers. There is no resolution. There is only a continuous development of an imperfect democracy to face the threats that are inherent in its foundations. Euripides acknowledges the relevance of Aeschylean justice. Seferis (1995), a modern Greek poet, continues in his poem "Mycenae" Aeschylus's and Euripides' tragic reading of history:

Sinks whoever raises the great stones;
I've raised these stones as long as I was able
I've loved theses stones as long as I was able
These stones, my fate
. . .
I know that they don't know, but I
who've followed so many times
the path from the killer to victim
from victim to punishment
from punishment to the next murder,
groping
the inexhaustible purple
that night of the return
when the Furies began whistling

The scholars observe: evil is not asleep, there is enough lament, enough pain to last a lifetime. In the foundations of democracy lies the source of the constant threat against its edifice, the destructive drives (Freud, 1920, 1930).[2]

Euripides hates war but accepts that the pleasure of destruction is inherent in human lives.[3] Greece is crazy for war. Humans are unable to ponder on their death.

HERALD: Don't trust in hope: it's sent many cities to war
whipping them into frenzy. Whenever war
comes up for the people's vote, no one counts on
his own death; each thinks the other man
will suffer. But if death rose before your eyes
when you cast your vote, Greece in its craze for spears
would not be destroyed in battle

[469–475]

. . . A hothead leader, a young captain,
spells danger. A man calm in crisis is wise.
In fact, courage truly defined is: foresight

[496–498]

Moderation is the true courage. Euripides realises that there is an innate
pleasure in the ruthless act of annihilating any object, any line of resistance,
any order and organisation. Restraining this primitive pleasure needs courage. Adrastos at the sight of the corpses cries for peace.

ADRASTOS: Tormented race of man,
Why do you take up spears, and bring down death
Upon each other? Stop! Leave off those labours,
Guard your city in peace. The needs of life
Are small. You should provide for them
Gently, without such gruesome labour

[904–9]

The Suppliants in pain also praise peace [1099–1101]. The voices of the
lamenting women are not silent, they assert their truth. The mothers of the
dead say no. No, nothing of what Adrastos has said in his funeral oration
could compensate for their children's deaths.

Rose (2018:17, 44, 117, 188) asked us to think about the mothers' position in
public life: The lamenting mothers are often used as hallmark images of disaster.
Their pain is often exploited in a policy that aims at making people emotional
without allowing them to hold accountable those who are responsible. Why is it
that because of the fact that they are mothers, we do not consider them capable
of contributing to the understanding and ordering of the public political space?
Euripides brings the mothers' lamenting voices into the political space of the
agora. Aithra makes her plea in the name of the city and on behalf of mothers
who are not her kin. She presents her case in terms of the contribution mothers
make to the civic good. She says in a way that we can take as model for our
social wellbeing the complex and painful reality of motherhood.

Memory or death

A helpless newborn baby is dependent for its survival on specific responses from its mother. It registers in its memory the experiences of life (immortality) when the mother is effective and the experiences of death (annihilation) when the mother fails (Freud, 1895 [1950]:297, 318, 366, 378). From the moment the child emerges as a subject, it struggles between memory and death. It enacts and repeats its experiences by the use of metaphors, endowing them with meaning and thus integrating them. It constantly registers stories and episodes of itself. It revives the present through the past. It differs from the animals because it tells stories. It becomes a hero of its adventures, undertaking the risks, e.g. of the impulses that threaten the survival of its objects. The adventures of interpreting the world and participation in it prepare the child for public life.

We are by nature political animals. Politics is a basic form of life, a game. We are alive, attending and participating in a shared world; when we play, we publicly express our innermost experiences. Then we live creatively, we do not conform. If we sacrifice our autonomy in order to adapt to the traumatic reality, we exist mechanically. We live a creative existence when we re-experience and re-constitute the past in the present (Winnicott, 1971; Parsons, 2014).

Parsons (2014) writes: The creative apperception gives meaning to the present in the light of the past. Après-coup gives fresh meaning to the past in the light of the present. Also it is essential that we enliven the present by the continual configuring of one's availability to the future. The present moment is then created by an unconscious encounter between après-coup and avant-coup.

Winnicott thought that apperception is the basis for creative living as opposed to a mechanical life of compliance. We can think of apperception as the mind perceiving itself as a subject of its own psychic states, which it lives by uniting past and present experiences. It integrates a present experience in the psychic history, and restores confidence in the state of the union, the coherence and the continuity, of the self and the polis.

The epic idea about immortality – where do the dead go – is given by Homer's poems (Jouanna, 2015). Tragedy brings up to date Homer's poems. It maintains epic elements about ethics. The Homeric idea that immortality is an affair for the living – those who remember, honour and tell stories about the life of the dead – makes sense to Euripides's audience and to us today. The idea is that death is contrasted to memory. It is a matter for the living to provide proper burial and mourning for the dead.

The work of mourning brings the future, endless repetitions bring eternity

The dead who is being mourned is the cause for the living to feel alive, get together, and speak. Poetry, politics, and religion meet in a final act, the funeral oration, a chance to form a "koinon" (common bond) among the citizens, who weave links of identification, share experiences and learn from them. It is not simply a matter of life and death. It is a matter of the dead person being preserved as a member of the human canon. It is unthinkable to disappear from the face of the earth, unable to be seen in the face of another person. The dead needs to be reflected in the eyes of their community. The mothers chant. They intone their unbearable pain in human time, rhythm, poetic meter. They call their sons out though they know they are dead and they say it. They say it with other grieving mothers, in common!

The dead person who is properly buried is the cause for time to move on to the future. Before being buried the dead are unfinished ghosts. The Suppliants wander off and finally arrive at a place, like Demeter, trying to locate them. After they are buried, the dead become lost children for their mothers, murdered fathers for their sons, abandoning husbands for their spouses. Finally, the dead suffer a second death. Then, their loss feels painfully real. With the internal acceptance of death, a definite separation is set up between the dead and the living.

Adrastos wishes to be united with the dead. He wishes to be swallowed up by the earth, torn apart by a whirlwind or stricken on the head by a thunderbolt from Zeus. The mothers who lost their children wish to die too along with their sons.

Iphis, in extreme pain, despises those who deny the passage of time and try to stay young forever with magic potions.

IPHIS: Old age, I despise this wrestle with you.
I despise those fools who coax out life's last days
with fancy diets and potions and witchery,
diverting life's course, trying to bypass death.
They ought, rather, when they're useless with old age,
To clear out the way and leave room for the young.

[1059–1064]

The monotonous lamentation aims at making eternal the time the mourners are with their dead, not wanting to let go and yet doing so in small dosages, accepting the painful reality. There are so many things they wished they had said to them. The wish for eternity is juxtaposed to the wish for immortality as is shown by the children's voices undertaking to convey the memory of the dead to the future.

CHORUS: I've dragged out too long a life,
melting, in grief after grief:
what greater grief can there be

for mortals, than to see
our own children, ash and bone.
CHILDREN: I bear them, I bear them –
Sad mother, I bear my father's bones from the flame.
So heavy they are, so weighted with grief, my whole
Life in a jar so small.
CHOROUS: Child, bring your beloved
mother these tears for the dead,
this small heap of ash, not the great
CHILDREN: You are childless, childless,
And I am torn from my father in distress,
In lonely hallways, orphaned,
Wrenched from my father's hand.
CHORUS: Where are the pangs of labor? The nights beguiled
By long watches over the sleeping child?
Where are the suckling, the rocking, the tenderness
Of kissing his sweet face?
CHILDREN: They are gone. Forever. My father-
They are gone-
CHORUS: – into air
Their bodies have melted into ash and fire,
To the Underworld they have flown

[1069–1095]

The work of mourning opens the space of the agora (of conflict)

The act of supplication was very important in ancient Greece from Homer to Euripides. The political supplication is a suitable occasion to present the distress of a helpless subject, who struggles to be in the world of others. The distress of the Suppliants reminds us of the helpless newborn infant who depends on the mother's support to continue living and growing. The political supplication anticipates that the mythic, mystical, religious "binding" will be transformed into a political commitment of the subjects of a state, which is "bound" by alliances of community.

The subject is faced with great resistance in meeting the immanent reality of the object. There is an immanent sense of impropriety when the "women of sorrow" intrude in the sacred space. What is immanent is the object, the other, who has meaning for the subject.

With the mourners' pain of loss, the Suppliants suddenly disrupt the divine fertility rite. A sacrosanct core is threatened. The continuity of a sacred process, the holding on to life, is threatened by the intrusion. When the mythic

and mystical order of the religious settings is disrupted, a new – political –
order begins to develop. The political evolves – is not dissociated – from
its mystical roots.

Rhem (2002:25) argues that in this play we see only arrivals from, and
departures to, various distant spaces.

> In the process, the play moves away from its Eleusinian setting and the
> promise of the Mysteries. . . . In its place, the political space of Athens
> increasingly dominates the action, culminating in the arrival of Athena,
> warrior goddess of the city, on the machine.

Eleusis is the suitable place to stage the plot of how politics are initiated
by the conflict between life and death forces. We can imagine that the fertility rites celebrate the union between goddess Demeter and her daughter,
Kore, the core of the mother's existence. Their mutual adaptation is a process bigger than the self, which holds the divinity of an isolated mysterious
living existence. The timeless peace of a primary un-integration (a mother-
child primary mutual autoerotic pleasure) as it is re-enacted in a fertility rite
is disturbed by the awareness of the urgency of time passage (integration
of reality).

Corpses left unburied disintegrate. Theseus is asked to tame this reality,
protect the integrity of the memory of the dead and separate them from the
living. He helps the grieving mothers leave their sons, to let them die, hand
them over to time. Politics is a work of culture that begins when the subject
separates from the primary unintegrated union; it undertakes the painful
mourning that facilitates the release of the investments for displacement in
new substitute objects. In order to agree to the reality (of loss), the subject
asks for compensation. The compensation is both a material thing and an
abstract symbolic opening of the horizon to personal and collective awareness. These exchanges are essential in the politics of a moderate democracy.
They balance contradictory demands.

> The poignancy of mourning and the simple eloquence of supplication
> yield to political discourse with a strong fifth-century accent. The sense
> that Athens has become the place of the play increases markedly with
> the release of Aithra from the suppliant bondage . . . the encounter
> between Theseus and the Theban Herald accelerates this transforma-
> tion. . . . The space of the play becomes increasingly reflexive, as the
> Eleusinian setting and its mythical associations fade. . . . More and
> more the theatre resembles an Athenian public forum.
>
> (Rhem, 2002:26–27)

The "weight" of the world

The dead are appropriated by the polis for the sake of its order. Theseus prohibits the lamenting mothers from touching the bodies of their dead sons. Their poignant craving for physical, intimate contact with their dead sons is left un-responded and weighs heavily inside them like a rock while they feel their selves becoming so light that they are lifted up in the air. They wish to be given their sons' bodies to hold, to make them their sons again. They do not want to feel alienated, remote strangers, rejected by their sons. They want to mourn and make the reality feel real.

ADRASTOS; Bring in the bodies, soaked in blood,
of those unlucky dead,
shamefully slain by the shameful
on whose battleground they fell.

[771–777]

"With this abrupt shift from the rhetoric of eulogy to the ugly facts of blood, wounds, and bodily decay, the pathos of loss resurges unabated, and remains unassuaged by the physical contact for which the mothers have longed" (Burian, 1985:147).

CHORUS: give him here, let me hold my boy
Folded in my embrace,
Let my hands caress his face
ADRASTOS; You hold, you hold-
CHORUS – the weight of the world

[775–780]

Our selves always become and exist in a state of fluidity. However, there is a rock of reality that remains unelaborated at the heart of every formation (psychic or social link of meaning) which we construct. Reality's bedrock is a metaphor for the untranslated experience. It is an image allowing us to think that there is always an aspect of the perception that cannot be elaborated.

A rock signifies something immovable, un-transformable, a fixed rigid integration that can only disintegrate. The perception that is left over, the remnant of reality that escapes the disintegration is what always returns and is used for finding and inventing the reality anew. The poets help us envelop in meaning the rock of reality and fit it in our stories.[4]

The tragedy here takes an intensely private form, but the public and political implications of extreme responses to loss are displayed in the startling second commos. The children of the Seven bear their fathers' ashes to the mourning mothers. For the mothers, this is the greatest pathos of all . . . they are numb from grief. . . . But the heroic impulse cannot be stilled, and it suddenly bursts forth from the children as a cry for vengeance.

(Burian, 1985:152)

CHILDREN: father, do you hear your children mourn?
Will I ever avenge your death with my own shield?
may that day come for your child'.
With god willing, we may win justice for our fathers.
CHOROUS: Enough pain!
Enough sorrow, enough
Fruitless grief.
CHILDREN: One day the River Asopus at Thebes will shine
and receive me as I march, leading the men of Argos
in bronze armor to avenge my father's loss
Father, you seem to hover before my eyes-
CHORUS: Leaning close to clasp and kiss-
CHILDREN: But your heartening message flies
into thin air and disappears.
CHORUS: He left a double grief: one for the mother.
one for the son who will grieve forever.
CHILDREN: The burden crushes out my life

[1094–1111]

The play goes on. The birth of children and the waging of war continue. When old Iphis exits, the grandsons take the stage promising to continue the war! What options are left for us?

Iphis left the scene to make way for the young, and the youths enter as if to confirm his bleak view of the human condition. The mothers for their part join the wish for vengeance . . . while at the same time they dread what the resurgence of bloodshed may bring.

(Burian, 1985:152)

We have two options: the work of mourning that gives us the future, the succession of time, the next generation who will continue our immortality; or the compulsion of repetition, which gives us the tyrannical feeling of eternity. Politics enables us to keep the faith to our immortality while we struggle to integrate and become the tragic subjects of our fate, responsible for the experiences we create and relive in the present and the meanings we give to them with our fantasies.

The time of separation, linear time

Euripides' Theseus, one of the few mythical heroes who descended to Hades, oversees the irreducible split between the living and the dead. Theseus stands on the living side of the split; on the side of the dead, Cerberus, the hound of Hades, guards the gates. Euripides introduces the most painful limit to the omnipotence of humans, the realisation of the linear flow of time, the time of separation. The mother is expected to let her child leave her behind. She gradually gives her child to time; the time that passes. The realisation of the flow of time calls for the work of mourning, that is, a conscious public process of accepting the reality that separates the dead from the living (Freud, 1915 [1917]:252; Ogden, 2002:778). The mourning process brings the future.

> . . . when the people rule their land
> they delight in the young men growing up
>
> [434–435]

Tyrants hate the next generation because it represents the passing of time. They kill the noble or smart youth in order to preserve their own reign, says Euripides in this play. We can associate this with the tyrants' manic refusal to allow the internal reality of loss and mourning to take place. They cannot make a tragic plot out of their lives. They cannot achieve a sense of the tragic; they cannot live inside time and die in time; they create real destruction in the world in order to be able to die themselves. They cannot conceive that they can die while the world continues to live.

By contrast, the chorus of the tragedy represents the democratic assembly of people, which discusses and researches a case concerning the city. The hypothesis of every research is concluded when the members of a plot meet in the same assembly, the same space. This gathering happens in the internal (re-membering) and also the external social reality (democratic process of civil participation). The positive side of this is the holding together of opposing, often contradictory elements, in a coherent whole, the polis, which is membered by subjects who think and have the sense of the tragic. The negative side is the fragmentation of the social fabric (dis-membering) into civil strife between families, factions and demes.[5]

The Suppliants begin with the right of the dead to die, be buried and escorted to death. The living enact their unassimilated experiences of loss, in order to mourn, symbolise, and integrate them in psychic life and in their collective history – and to reconcile with them. The ghosts (shadows of lost objects wandering homeless without full existence across generations) take on symbolic forms and cease to haunt the living; they become memories, which are recognised, recollected, and contained in psychic space. With each step of representation and internalisation of the unassimilated traces of experience, new connections are created that increase the capacity of the network of exchanges between internal and external reality.

Adrastos, full of pain, mourns the dead. In a despairing speech he declares that he desires to die along with them. This is an excruciating act of identification with the dead; to become a ghost himself, to leave life, like the dead left him, and accompany them to the bed of fire where they lie incredibly alone, unaccompanied, inaccessible. By contrast, Theseus is alive, present, serving in an official capacity. His public function is to separate between the dead and the living and build bridges of living memories between them. He makes mourning an affair of the polis that creates links of freedom between the living. The joy of life is a shared ideal, a legitimate manic defence that needs to be defended by the laws.

The play itself is an open-ended process that provides the linear movement of time – the time of separation and mourning, the time of integration, and the sense of irreversibility that makes life move on to the next objects. It helps the subject to not be devastated, but to tolerate the reality; it feels unbearably painful now but it is not the end of the world and will not last for an eternity. The play anticipates the future. The individuals hold the time needed for the meaning of loss to be formed so as to make acceptable the sense of transience. The subject is then a matter of time, a being that goes on, a continuity of time (Manolopoulos, 2003).

For the subject to allow the dead to die and time to move on there needs to be an exchange of the loss for a new real pleasure, a substitute, and the freedom that the future brings. The written oaths that bind the allies, the tripod at Delphi and the buried knife in Eleusis, together with the promise of justice in future revenge by the sons are the substitutes for the loss of the fathers, terminating this episode of mourning, placing the subjects inside reality and time, and allowing life to go on.

What matters are the continuity of the living process and the links of community, where experiences are created and shared as a source of learning. However, there always remain many compromises as well as uncompromised contradictions. Many unresolved galaxies of subjectivity are still in the universe. Mourning lasts a lifetime and is transmitted to the next generation.

Winnicott (1963b:93–94) assumes that man "continues to create and re-create God as a place to put that which is good in himself, and which he might spoil if he kept it in himself along with all the hate and destructiveness which is also to be found there". This is why moral education persists.

The educative funeral speech of Adrastos assigns the dead to a place where they shall be forever dead and benevolent ancestors, not angry demons, carriers of projected hate. They become a protective place where people trust the unity of their polis.

Earthly immortality

Psychoanalysis has found in ancient tragedy the theatre of everyday life that enables us to put in our minds the unthinkable of which we are deeply aware. We are compelled to internalise it notwithstanding the fear involved. Then, "we can understand the gripping power of Oedipus Rex, in spite of all the objections that reason raises against the presupposition of fate" (Freud, 1897:223).

One becomes a leader when one dares to know the answer to things unknown. Oedipus struggles to know why the plague has visited Thebes; he wants to know who is responsible, he wants to know himself. Not everybody attains the capability of separation, mourning, the Oedipal complex, the sense of reality.

A father who is killed becomes god and a totemic animal victim, triumphant in the end. He then becomes god and king, whose authority is defined by voluntary obedience and freedom, by commitment instead of submission that corresponds to perpetual guilt and rebellion by the sons. (Freud, 1912–13:151). The work of mourning and oedipal complex is the peak of infantile sexuality in the tragic way of internalisation and succession (Suljagic, 2016).

Green (1980) notes: Theseus had a god for father, Poseidon, and an earthly father, Aegeus, whom he was trying to deny. The meeting with Oedipus made Theseus forsake divinity and choose to live on the earth. By assuming man's fate, Theseus became an exemplar of what he was struggling to become the subject of. He chose to re-enact, transform, and integrate his omnipotence, bisexuality, and impulses. He chose to live within time. In contrast to the other great hero Heracles, whose sexuality is more metaphorical, Theseus abducts the Amazon Antiope and has a child with her. His act is less symbolic and more human. It gives vent to the gratification of impulses. The incursion of the Amazons, who push as far as the very heart of Athens, occurs after the reforms instituted by the civilising Theseus. The invasion of the Amazons poses a threat to the return of those forces that had been expelled with the reformation. The meeting of Theseus with Oedipus simply makes all his triumphs humane, observes Gide.

In the Suppliants is not Oedipus who comes to the outskirts of Athens but Adrastos accompanying the Suppliant Women in search of a burial place for their sons. Oedipus goes to the holy place of the Furies (*Erinyes, Ἐρινύες*) at Colonus, looking to find in Theseus a son who would "kill" him, an eyewitness to his death, the one who would know him. Adrastos is looking for a son to store the memory and then tell the story. He is searching for a son to succeed him, to grant him immortality.

> The task and potential greatness of mortals lie in their ability to produce things – works and deeds and words – which would deserve to be and, at least to a degree, are at home in everlastingness, so that through them mortals could find their place in a cosmos where everything is immortal except themselves. By their capacity for the immortal deed, by their ability to leave non-perishable traces behind, men, their individual mortality notwithstanding, attain an immortality of their own and prove themselves to be of a "divine" nature.
>
> (Arendt, 1958:19)

Faith in immortality is what the polis needs. Faith in immortality preserves the significance of history and topography of public life, the integrity of the polis. The wish for immortality must exist in the foundation of the city. The world lasts beyond our finite lifetime, it is made of the stories that make the dead parents immortal ancestors for having performed heroic actions. Our heroes make the common history understandable. Their stories inspire us to assert our fundamental right to be seen and heard and get responses that matter in the present along with symbolic meanings that unlock the future. In contrast, the wish for eternity does not lead us towards any action.

Sklar (2018) examined these conditions for the work of mourning and symbolisation of traumatic experiences that make room for freedom to think and speak and act on behalf of the future for the children of the world.

Theseus meets Oedipus in Athenian myths and politics

The myths of the Suppliants and Oedipus show an evolution towards the foundation of the realm of politics. Forced by the epidemic that erupted in Thebes, Oedipus began to search for the cause, only to turn inside him in order to discover and internalise his fantasies of omnipotence, his bisexuality and his drives; in the end he became a subject accountable for them, a truly tragic, political, subject.

Beyond the political order lies an untamed land populated with early unsymbolised experiences that are organised with deep irreducible splits, the archaic logic of which the tragic poets help us to understand. Out of the horror of the abyss, humans create the horrible Sphinx as a permanent habitat of the splits of psychic and social life. The Sphinx was killed once by Oedipus, but it came back in the form of an epidemic that killed the ignorant and the arrogant. Sphinx, a prehistoric monster, is our gate to primordial anxieties of extinction in a black hole. We can think that this black hole is transformed into a secret place of Oedipus' ascension, on which the power of the leaders of Athens is founded.

Oedipus' time had come but he had no place to die. In Athens, Oedipus was granted asylum by Theseus. Athens had the fortitude to provide a hospitable place; it dared to integrate split-off primitive elements.

Parsons (1990:40) examines how in Euripides's *Bacchae* and Sophocles' *Oedipus at Colonus* the ruler of a city is confronted with a stranger: a dangerous figure, imbued with sacred meaning, who demands recognition.

> Dionysos can be seen as an aspect of Pentheus's own personality which he has split off and rejected, and similarly with Oedipus and Theseus. Pentheus and Oedipus are faced with the same demand to acknowledge something in themselves, which they have found intolerable and avoided knowing about. The outcome of each play shows how Theseus achieves this task while Pentheus is unable to do so.

Theseus accompanied Oedipus to the secret place of his ascension. Only Theseus knew this place, and he was allowed to reveal it only to his own successor. Each new leader of Athens knew the secret place, and from this knowledge he derived his power and undertook on behalf of the people the immortality project (the achievements for which they will be remembered) of each generation. No citizen knew the location where Oedipus was buried. It is a no-place. It is up in the air. The political order is based on the oedipal situation.

A single people in one city

In an episode of the myth, Theseus falls into deep sorrow when a rival of his, who was rejected by the Amazon Antiope, kills himself. The association to his father's death is clear. Theseus recalled an oracle of Pythia telling him that when he experiences deep sorrow he should build a city on the particular site, leaving some of his comrades to govern it. Here the myth links the mourning to the founding of the city. Theseus hands over to the people a system of government without a king and resigns. The sense of guilt towards the dead father after the patricide leads Theseus to contribute to society through the reforms he introduces to the city. However, a pre-Oedipal interpretation is needed here towards the mother's side. He fights against rifts and divisions among the families, factions and municipalities. The aim is to unite them "in a single people in one city". The brothers agree among themselves (union and uniformity of the laws and institutions) that the mother-city would not belong to anyone. This reform means the reunification of the dismembered maternal body. It has to do with the mother and the children, the city and the citizens (Green, 1980).

Politics is based on the ability to live within time with a simultaneous belief in immortality. We make political decisions within time, time that follows a flow towards the end. At the same time we live in the timelessness, where the memories of experiences are continually stratified to form new webs of meaning and new stories that are differentiated and integrated anew.

At Colonus Oedipus heard the roar of thunder and lightning – a divine omen that the time of death had come. He took with him Theseus as witness to show only him the site of his death. Only the ruler and his successors are destined to know. The site of his death becomes a place where immortality is guarded as the secret of existence by the rulers and passed on to the city.

At the end of his life, he comes to the conclusion of his tragic hypothesis with a revelation: The primal scene that brought the individual to life and the death that took him away are two occurrences which are forever unknown. It is a time and place where it is impossible for one to be present as subject and live the experience. The secret of existence is guarded by the prophets, the poets and the leaders, those who respect the necessity of the fate, the continuance of the nether and upper worlds, the unconscious and the conscious.

There is no end to our thinking; we continue to transform reality up until life's end. We do not attain absolute knowledge. The thing in itself is unknowable. We always doubt if what we are thinking inside us corresponds to something perceptible in reality. We also need good luck. This uncertainty sets a limit to our omnipotence. This is the essence of democracy. We think, and in this way of thinking and based on the particular thought, we reach our decisions, be what they may, at our own peril.

Participation in social life

Winnicott (1963a) – following Melanie Klein's great contribution to our understanding of the integration processes – considers that our participation in social life is a major accomplishment of the work of mourning. In the beginning of life the environment-mother trades with the child mutual tenderness, sensual and emotional coexistence, while the object-mother becomes the target for his instinctual drives. When the child realises that these two functions of the mother come from the same person, he starts on the work of mourning, going through the depressive position that results in the capacity to feel guilt and concern.

Winnicott (1948:96) also examines how people use a social group for a reparation activity in respect of a common pool of guilt: Each member contributes to the group's restitution urge, which relates to the group's depressive anxieties. But this restitution in the group must wait on more important thing. Each individual must develop his *own* sense of responsibility based truly on personal guilt and concern about his own impulses and their consequences.

Someone may be reluctant to participate in society for fear of getting caught again in the anti-depressive defences of his mother. By contrast, Theseus was eager to become involved in his city's affairs. His mother's name, Aithra, meaning "clear sky" in Greek, reminds us of the work of mourning that clears away the fog of depression and sharpens the sense of reality and time.

Castoriadis (1999) pointed out that democracy for the Athenians was a "tragic" regime. Tragedy is a political institution. It reminds the Athenians that there are a priori unknown limits to the subject, who acts by undertaking the risks and the responsibility of their thoughts and actions. Democracy is a regime of freedom but also of subjectivation (internalisation) and responsibility.

Parsons (2016:23) thought of the True Self as described by Winnicott, and the "subject" as theorised in French psychoanalysis, as representing an authentic conscience, which allows us to become the authors of our own authority. Totalitarian external authorities fear and hate the authority of the true self.

Being a subject means being able to achieve a sense of the tragic. It means that one integrates aspects of the self that he is compelled to relive in the present. He is present for the experiences to happen to him. He undertakes personally the responsibility of the meanings he gives them. Hitler could not achieve a sense of the tragic, he could not make a tragic plot, internalising his madness; he created real destruction in order to be able to live in time and die. In contrast, Prospero could live his tragedy and attain the capacity to be mortal (Manolopoulos, 2016:32).

The subject is a layering of ongoing transcriptions and re-transcriptions of memories, which we revisit in the present. The tragic subject is a capacity to think. It is made of stories that need other selves – who reflect back the investments – in order to be spoken and acted in public. The essence of this process is the metaphoric speech that links meanings with bodily experiences and makes the dream, the play, the transference and the theatre a therapeutic medium. The art of politics is part of such a healing work afforded by culture in a democratic polis.

Notes

1 "ἀφῖγμαι δ᾽ ἐκ θεοῦ μυστηρίων Ἀργεῖον οὖδας οὐδενὸς ξυνειδότος, φόνον φονεῦσι πατρὸς ἀλλάξων ἐμοῦ" (Euripides' Electra [89] in Kovacs, 1998:159–160).

2 Freud (1920:45) quoted Schiller, another poet-philosopher, who, like Euripides, recognised with a deep awareness of the dark violent forces, the humans' struggle "to bear the burden of existence".

3 Thucydides' history (Book 1, 1,8) proves that every polis which thinks itself more powerful will always fight to dominate any other which is weaker.

4 The image of a rock is often used in the play. For example, the rock of Eleutherai is the site on mount Kithairon where Theseus buried the common soldiers of the Argive army; also, on a rock of the cliff above the stage stood Evadne before she leapt into the pyre. Finally, on this same rock Athena stood in the place of Evadne, to speak the last word of truth on politics.

5 Thucydides [3.82.2] reminds us that civil strife will continue since human nature remains unchanged (ἕως ἂν ἡ αὐτὴ φύσις ἀνθρώπων ᾖ).

References

Arendt H. (1958) *The Human Condition*. Chicago, Chicago University Press.

Burian P. (1985) Logos and Pathos: The Politics of the Suppliant Women. In P. Burian (Ed.) *Directions in Euripidean Criticism: A Collection of Essays*. Durham, NC, Duke University Press.

Castoriadis C. (1999) *The Ancient Greek Democracy and Its Significance for Us Today*. In Greek. Athens, Ypsilon.

Euripides'. (1995) *Suppliant Women*. (Trans. R. Warren and S. Scully). Oxford, Oxford University Press.

Foley P. H. (2001) *Female Acts in Greek Tragedy*. Princeton, Princeton University Press.

Freud S. (1895 [1950]) Project for a Scientific Psychology. *S.E.*, *1*.

———. (1897 [1954]) Letter to Wilhelm Fliess of 15th October 1897: Letter 71. In *The Origins of Psycho-Analysis: Letters to Wilhelm Fliess, Drafts and Notes, 1887–1902*. (Trans. E. Mosbacher and J. Strackey). London, Imago.

———. (1912–1913) Totem and Taboo: Some Points of Agreement between the Mental Lives of Savages and Neurotics. *S.E.*, *13*.

———. (1915 [1917]) Mourning and Melancholia. *S.E.*, *14*.

———. (1920) Beyond the Pleasure Principle. *S.E.*, *18*.

———. (1930) Civilization and Its Discontents. *S.E.*, *21*.

Green A. (1980) Thésée et Oedipe. Une iterprétation psychanalytique de la Thésé-ide. In *Psychanalyse et Culture Greque. Confluents Psychanalytique*. Paris, Les Belles Lettres. In Greek (Trans. M. Fragopoulos). Athens, Rappa (1985).

Jouanna D. (2015) *Les Greecs aux Enfers. D'Homère a Épicure*. Paris, Les Belles Lettres. In Greek (Trans. H. Magoulas, Ed. S. Metevelis). Athens, Estia (2019).

Kovacs D. (1998) *Euripides: Suppliant Women, Electra, Heracles*. Cambridge, MA, Harvard University Press.

Loraux N. (2002) *The Mourning Voice: An Essay on Greek Tragedy*. London, Cornell University Press.

Manolopoulos S. (2003) The Sense of Transience in Transferential and Transitional Phenomena. *Israel Psychoanalytic Journal*, *1*(2), 225–245.

————. (2016) Discussion of Michael Parsons' Paper. *Psychoanalysis in Europe, EPF Bulletin*, *70*, 29–34.

Ogden T. (2002) A New Reading of the Origins of Object-Relations Theory. *International Journal of Psycho-Analysis*, *83*(4), 767–782.

Parsons M. (1990) Self-Knowledge Refused and Accepted. *Journal of Analytic Psychology*, *35*(1), 19–40.

————. (2014) *Why Did Orpheus Look Back? Après-coup, avant-coup. Living Psychoanalysis*. London and New York, Routledge.

————. (2016) Authors of Our Own Authority. *Psychoanalysis in Europe, EPF Bulletin*, *70*, 19–28.

Rhem R. (2002) *The Play of Space: Spatial Transformation in Greek Tragedy*. Princeton and Oxford, Princeton Universities Press.

Rose J. (2018) *Mothers: An Essay on Love and Cruelty*. London, Faber & Faber.

Scully S. (1995) Introduction. In *Euripides, Suppliant Women* (Trans. Rosanna Warren and Stephen Scully). Oxford, Oxford University Press.

Seferis G. (1995) II Mycenae, Oct. 1935. In *George Seferis Complete Poems* (Trans. E. Keeley and P. Sherrard). London, Carcanet Classics.

Sklar J. (2018) *Dark Times: Psychoanalytic Perspectives on Politics, History, and Mourning*. London, Phoenix Publishing House.

Storey C. (2008) *Euripides: Suppliant Women*. London, Duckworth.

Suljagic J. (2016) The Many Facets of Authority in Psychoanalytic Institutions (unpublished paper). Available at: www.epf-fep.eu/eng/article/the-many-facets-of-authority-in-psychoanalytic-institutions (requires login).

Thucydides'. (1910) *The Peloponnesian War*. London, J. M. Dent; New York, E. P. Dutton.

Winnicott D. (1948 [1992]) Reparation in Respect of Mother's Organized Defence against Depression. In *Through Paediatrics to Psychoanalysis*. London, Karnac Books.

————. (1963a [1990]) The Development of the Capacity for Concern. In *The Maturational Processes and the Facilitating Environment*. London, Karnac Books.

————. (1963b [1990]) Morals and Education. In *The Maturational Processes and the Facilitating Environment*. London, Karnac Books.

————. (1971) *Playing and Reality*. London, Tavistock.

4   The feminine core

Sotiris Manolopoulos

In Euripides' *Suppliants*, men dominate the political stage. However, the women know the story and intervene at crucial moments to change its plot. We can now think about a feminine intelligence that lies at the foundation of the polis.

Iphis reminds us: femininity is a riddle [1064].

Femininity is the most feared and repudiated element in both sexes (Freud, 1937a:250). Winnicott (1950:251–252) argues that all men and women have in common a fear of WOMAN, which is a powerful agent in society's structure.

> The root of this fear . . . is related to the fact that in early history of every individual who develops well . . . there is debt to a woman – the woman who was devoted to that individual as an infant, and whose devotion was absolutely essential for that individual's healthy development. The original dependence is not remembered and therefore the debt is not acknowledged, except in so far as the fear of woman represents the first stage of this acknowledgment.

These original exchanges between infant and mother, the primary and secondary, narcissistic and oedipal identifications with mother and father, are inscribed in infancy. They form a core feminine "intelligence".

"Euripides felt, and for any thinking member of his audience he taught, a supreme compassion for the painful precariousness of the human condition; and he taught it most of all through his women characters" (March, 1990:63). Euripides is not a misogynist.

Mendelsohn (2002:49) argues that the poet's

> tragic theorizing is nonetheless striking in its attempt to infect patriarchy with the feminine, to suggest that ideology imposes itself at a considerable price. Any attempt to construct a space that is wholly uninfected by

DOI: 10.4324/9781003252184-5

the assumptions that underpin one's own cultural discourse – patriarchy, imperialism, even democracy – is, after all, doomed; but it is an attempt surely worthy of note.

An interpretative strategy that aims to integrate fully both the feminine and the political in Euripides' two political plays seems not only welcome but appropriate. The *Suppliants* is a drama that is realised in a place where the processes of the feminine and mourning are everywhere (Mendelsohn, 2002:28, 135).

(Re)casting of the female

Athenians in the fifth century still showed to the visitors of their city the place where the Amazons were buried, as archaic elements that lie at the polis' foundations. They were afraid and wished that these elements might wake up.

Petrou (2019) takes an anthropological and psychoanalytic stand in order to examine the "theory" of matriarchy (mythical belief that in the dawn of civilisation authority was in the hands of women). He explains: The belief of a passage from matriarchy to patriarchy is upheld as an event of the evolution that is repeated in the development of the infant, who moves from the dual relationship with the mother towards the triangular relationship that includes the authority of the father. Freud (1939:82–85) believed in the theory of matriarchy, female governance, as a social system and an evolutionary stage of humanity. He thought that the move from matriarchy to patriarchy is a victory of intellectuality over sensuality. However, the theory of matriarchy has been rejected by ethnological and archaeological research.

The myth of matriarchy persists because it is formed on the prototype of children's sexual theories about our origins. The fantasy of the total surrender to a powerful woman or the urgent need of the indisputable possession of the maternal space persist in public life. Potamianou (1996) examined the Greek myths that represent the absence of any deficiency. In Greek mythology the maternal world is the bearer of life and also of death. The maternal pole governs everything given to humans, even life and death, as Freud (1913) said in his "Theme of three caskets".

In ancient Athens women are absent as natural persons but they are very much present as social representations (Loraux, 1986). Euripides dramatises this absence-presence, silence-speech, inaction-action of women. The chorus of the *Suppliants* intervenes at crucial moments and takes an active public role. When the debate between Theseus and Adrastos reaches an impasse, Aithra goes public. Following Adrastos' funeral oration, the mothers of the chorus make their mourning public again. After Theseus forbids the touching of the dead bodies by the mothers, Evadne appears making a public statement; she is united with her dead husband. When, in the end, Theseus and Adrastos reach an agreement, Athena appears in public to tell the truth.

Euripides dramatises such logic of (re)casting as a return of split elements of femininity. Although the play moves from the religious institutions (fertility and mourning rites performed by women) to the political spaces (assembly, operated by men), there is always a public return of the women.

The primary mystery

We are at the place of the Eleusinian Mysteries, a site of many associations regarding the origins of life. The Greek words for "*mysteries*" (*μυστήρια*), "*mystic*" (*μύστης*), "*initiation*" (*μύησις*), and "*secret*" have a common etymological root, the word "*μύω*" (myo), which means we keep eyes and mouth shut when confronted with something awesome.[1]

The initiated in the Eleusinian Mysteries conquer death by submerging in the depths of existence and coming into contact with something that can neither be known nor remembered, or in any way reproduced. This is the sacred union of the infant with the primary mother, the feminine element of being, and the unknown underworld of early exchanges of humans with their primary environment. Only the initiated can access the Mysteries and they then keep silent. They ought to keep the secret of the unknown inside.

Primary experiences are out there somewhere, an unknown process that holds the secret of the continuity of existence, a meaning that lies at the heart of one's life story. What goes on in the mysteries is unknown. This non-awareness may represent the situation in which the infant's continued existence is absolutely dependent on maternal care, albeit knowing nothing about it (Winnicott, 1960:307).

A core of primary femininity is formed, as a foundation of being. It originates in the primary sensuality shared by the bodies of mother and the infant. It originates in an extreme asymmetry between a helpless infant facing death and the mother's responses. The infant literally survives only because the mother's mysterious "magic" responses to its gestures are adequate. Their exchanges save the existence from the agony of extinction. Links of memory about their exchanges are inscribed. The infant is unintegrated at first and needs a phase of holding as part of maternal care, in order to go on being, not yet able to tell the ego from the non-ego. In this phase, primary (processes, identifications, symbolism, autoerotism, narcissism) elements of experience sustain the continuity of being. The infant relies on suitable maternal responses to gradually achieve a state of integration of the ego and then be able to send a signal of anxiety, organise defences, and experience conflicts.

Ethics (and by extension politics) originate in the mother's response to her emerging infant's signals with a specific action that gives them the value of communication (Freud, 1895 [1950]:297, 318, 366, 378). The links of unity between an infant and its primary mother are sacred in all societies.

These early processes of linking maintain their sacred nature throughout life, both in the internal and external realities. The sacred nature of this unity is defended in the dramas of supplication with whatever means necessary, even war.

The work of psychic constructions, that is, linking, forming unities, transforming meanings of experiences, inscribing them in layers of memory, and integrating them, contains all along the negative aspect of the primitive ruthless pleasure, dissolving any line of differentiation, and destroying any structure.

The processes of integration begin from incorporations of concrete elements (hidden in the dark depths of the maternal body) to internalizations of abstract symbolic ones (bringing to life the light of fertility).

Moreover, keeping a secret is an integral part of the mystery of femininity, protecting the unknown depth of the female body where life is initiated, gestated and, in due course, born. The core of existence should be guarded as an isolated, hidden, non-communicable, sacred area. By not respecting this secret truth, not keeping a distance from the emerging true self, by intruding, the external reality of the object causes a major threat against the sense of existence, a disturbance of the sense of time and space, a threat against identity, a sense of depersonalisation.

The mysteries happen at the boundaries where transgressive leaps (separating and linking of different realms of realities) occur. The mysteries are protected by means of defined settings so that the external reality of the object does not invade the sense of the self in a traumatic way. The origins, the core of the self, are a sacred mystery and cannot be directly communicated (Winnicott, 1960:46–47, 1965:189).

We can think here that when the "reality of the object is imminent," it causes the fear of truth being exposed and raises resistance. There are occasions "when it is felt to be wise, not pathological, to turn a 'blind eye'" (Bion, 1965:147, 149). Hiding in the face of a predator is a normal defence for the preservation of the species. The art of dissimulation and deception is the means to preserve the weaker animals like humans. The ultimate refuge is a state of merger, something that groups seek in their regressions.

The evolution of this normal defence takes the form of compromising, and forging community alliances that safeguard the narcissism of the subject and his group. In periods of transition, a polis should resist assuming a rigid, sharply differentiated point of view in its politics. It needs, instead, the ethics of sympathy, friendship, and pity; it needs also to respond to the supplication of strangers with sympathy.

However, even a type of attitude of the softest transitional object presents an unyielding line of resistance, the truth of otherness, which raises primitive ruthless attacks to destroy it. The survival of the polis makes it external, and the attacking (the suppliant) stranger a subject of it. Euripides warns us that the transitional objects and the defences we use to form community alliances, can be perverted either by populist demagogues who promise that the infantile illusion of union can be a reality, or by the manic, war crazy, hawkish fanatics. Without sympathy towards the people's struggles, any institution becomes stupid, ridiculous and paranoid.

The primary creativity

In the *Suppliants*, behind the orchestra is situated the *skene*, the stage-building, and further behind a more remote space that cannot be seen. We can imagine that this represents the unknown interior of the mother's body full of mysteries, the secret source from where the unexpected ominous new things come to the light. We may surmise that the polis has a body of society with an unknown hidden space full of mysterious processes whereby myriads everyday life interactions take place. In order to be in contact with this secret internal space and to facilitate the potential of its development, we need the transitional phenomena of religion, poetry and politics, which make a movement geared towards an objective. This movement is always incomplete.

The orchestra in an ancient theatre is a space between internal and external reality, a place where the private has given up part of its room to make a shared public space, wherein the multiplicity and complexity of the links of the chorus and the actions of the protagonists in the play are contained and surrounded by us, the audience. The public is inside the private and the private inside the public.

In religion, art and politics we can see the integration of femininity in the capacity of humans to be passive – receptive and internalise new experiences while learning from them. We see the failure of integration of femininity in the fear of passivity, and in the anti-cathexes of phallic narcissistic despotic attacks on links of friendship and pity. If primary identifications fail in an extreme way, there is a deep irreducible split in the go of an individual and an unresolved conflict between the need and the fear (resulting in refusal) of internalisation, fear of submission (surrender) to others, and refusal of commitment.

In the *Suppliants* art, like religion, which it replaces, forges links of meaning and makes a "koinonia" out of the individuals. Theatre is a space to be and belong to, a process larger than life; it is a bigger power that holds the world; it makes no demand on you. Politics, like religion and the theatre, imitate the human primary creativity: a capacity for apperception, a capacity to perceive creatively the reality (Winnicott, 1971:65).

In the *Suppliants* the question is not how to win a contest but how to continue the play. The play is politics, that is, a process of successive events, which stages unresolved, unassimilated past experiences in the present for re-interpretation. Politics is presented as a drama with a rhythm, inherent music, surprising turns, sudden presentations of the future, and an unknown outcome.

Taming the supernatural forces is the role of the leader, who holds magically the rhythm of the world and promises immortality to his polis. The question each time is whether politics can contain a process in which the conflicts create a tragic plot that can be terminated. The problem is the interminable, stagnated non-process, where nothing new happens and fantasies of omnipotence fill the void. This is the adverse aspect of politics, the negative politics of a populist or totalitarian state which destroys the process whereby the individual is allowed to become a subject that understands and participates equally and effectively in what goes on.

The question is if someone will appear on stage willing and competent to undergo this process and become its subject, thus assuming the responsibility for the actions and the fantasies that constitute his polis each time. Each episode of the process ends when the symbolisation opens to a future horizon, an open-ended space and time, a wisdom that is called the order of the political. This willing and competent person, who accepts becoming part of their story, is someone the Suppliants are looking for.

Theseus, the hero of the myth, becomes a model for bravery. He gives us courage to stand up and face the contemporary dictators of cruelty, fanaticism, racism, misogyny. Theseus, the hero of the tragedy, undertakes personally the process that would change him. He gives us a position to stand as subjects and think.

The *Suppliants* taught Theseus the necessity to keep contact with the unruly reality of his feminine core, the anarchic primary autoerotic sexuality, while undergoing the painful work of mourning. He wandered all over Greece with his friend Peirithous, whose name is derived from the verb perithein (περιθείν) which means "to run around", and also "to move to and fro" when it is used to describe a warrior's shield. Theseus was a warrior who was capable of friendship and openness. He could be feminine-receptive, suffer his passion, interact with his objects and lose his way, his direction. He became a separate subject who could think, feel pity, and innovate.

What do the Suppliants look for at Eleusis?

The Suppliants seek to find a site representing the place where their children were lost; a site for their sons to appear for the last time; a stage to localise the last place where they were seen alive, before they disappeared from life. They struggle to lay to final rest their dearly beloved objects. They struggle to take in the bodies of their lost children, not the void of their loss. They ultimately look for their sons' sons to be the Epigonoi, to take their dead fathers' place, to form the narcissistic contract with their society, to be their future voice.

The Suppliants mourn their motherhood and re-live their ancient mourning, which they first went through in their own infancy when they separated from their own mothers. They re-enact and internalise the space (of femininity addressed to mother and father) where the child reigns as the third party. This internalisation can only be completed through the mothers' painful work of mourning for the loss of their children and the process of symbolisation. The Suppliants' "labour" is linked to childbirth. The pain to grow a child and the pain to lose one in a war makes mothers wish they never had given birth to children.

CHORUS: Child, it was for doom
I carried you in my womb;
and labored in Herculean pain
Now death takes as his spoil
the fruit of my laboring toil:
I am aged, untended, alone,
though I begot a son.

[872–878]

A little girl needs to take a decisive step away from the mother to move towards the father (changing her object of love). The mourning of losing the mother is a complex and painful process for a woman to bear and it leaves a melancholic mark of disappointment in her psyche. We usually talk about Demeter's mourning when she lost her daughter Kore, the core of her feminine existence. We forget the mourning that the daughter had to go through, to be liberated from the life in Hades, a world that is closed from everywhere, a world full of shadows of lost objects.

The Homeric Hymn to Demeter portrays a deep understanding of the female experience, and the significance of the mother-daughter bond in human nature and polis (Foley, 1994). In the return of her daughter, Demeter relives the joy of her bond with her own mother. Zeus sends Rhea to persuade Demeter. Demeter's closeness to her own mother brings her pleasure, and only then the earth's fertility returns. The line of three generations of women represents femininity. The Mysteries separate human from the divine world, but the idealization of the mother-daughter relationship is preserved.

We forget that a woman is also a daughter (Kore) who lost her mother, when she exited from the infantile oral/anal passivity towards her, in which she struggled to become autonomous. Her exodos towards freedom and the autonomy of her own body are not an easy task. Inherent in identifications of the girl with her mother is both an essential primary enjoyment (a sensual pleasurable free exchange) and a fundamental disappointment (Denis, 1982; Chabert, 2019).

At Eleusis, the Suppliant women ask for the wisdom of the feminine element of being, the negative capacity to abstract from the universe of passivity a capacity to be passive and receptive; to tolerate and accept the inevitability of the reality of the object; to transform reality and form alliances with confidence, obey the law without fear of surrendering to others.

The play concludes with the goddess of wisdom, Athena, inviting the Athenians to create meeting places with allies, creative spaces and times of focused attention. The goddess instructs citizens to focus on politics as an art that links internal and external events in mutual information and signification.

In the *Suppliants* we observe a dramatisation of the creation of religious, theatrical and political meeting places, out of the space that is created between the body of the mother and that of the infant when they separate. Public life requires the embodied presence of the participants in the same space where exchanges of verbal and extra verbal signs create and convey meaning.

Mendelsohn (2002:36–37) underlines the prominent role played by place, space and location: These unities give the play structural and thematic coherence.

> Each locale has a special meaning that can, as it were, be excavated; each affects our reading of the actions that transpire in them. For each there was a real place constituted by boundaries and borders, which played a role in Athenian history and, therefore, Athenian civic ideology". . . . But for every place . . . there is a "dis-place": well defined boundaries imply (indeed, almost invite) crossings, transgression.

An appreciation of these places and displacements – geographical and ritual, real and symbolic – is critical for our understanding of the play.

The Eleusinian setting of the *Suppliant's* mourning is the place of Demeter's wanderings. Finally, mother and daughter arrive at a place where they can separate and co-exist. This is the site where a poignant separation between mother and daughter took place. In there, Demeter found her lost daughter after she ascended from her husband's dark palace.

The place of death of the Seven and the retrieval of their dead bodies is located outside the walls of the desired city. Eleusis is the place of their burial. The dead are buried and thus they find a place to be separate and co-exist in memory with the living. The funeral oration gives them a space: to be dead and be mortal again in everyday exchanges; to be accompanied to the unknown mystery.

Theatre space holds the drama that begins and ends at Eleusis. It creates a political space of struggling to link: famine and feeding earth, need and love, loss and incorporation of the dead, arrogance and learning, death and memory, trap and commitment, femininity and freedom, mourning and politics, sanctuary and agora.

The Suppliant mothers go to Eleusis looking for a site to keep alive the memory of their sons. They seek to chart the ambiguous area that death leaves behind, to make it objective and give it the space of a representation, a place to contain it in memory. They finally give the place where their sons' sons, the Epigonoi, will stand, looking for their future integration in their primary paternal identifications.

What does it mean to be free? [429]

The struggling heroic father of prehistory (Theseus, Herakles), is a figure for future integration, for the children to find their own place in the world (Freud, 1921). He introduces them in the public domain. Theseus is the pre-historic founding father of the city of Athens. The father of a myth, a figure of imagination, Theseus is the great warrior, the ideologist and reformer (*ekpolitistis, ἐκπολιτιστής*) who brought civilisation.

Green (1980) in following Theseus in his mythical routes (Plutarch, XXII) reads the connection of mourning and femininity to politics: Theseus appropriates the power, the thread of thought of Ariadne, and frees himself from her dominance. After abandoning Ariadne he bursts on the island of Delos into a frenzied dance, which is a mimetic representation of the Labyrinth's spinning cycles at a rhythm of successive alternating movements and spiralling thrusts. Under the influence of this intoxicating dance, Theseus forgot to change the colour of the sails from black to white, causing his father to commit suicide by falling from the cliff of Poseidon's temple at Sounio. The deliverance of exiting the Labyrinth gives Theseus a particular individuality. The exodos resembles a new birth. Theseus frees the children from the pre-Oedipal Labyrinth. On his return to Athens he introduces the feast of the Oskhoforia (*ὀσχοφόρια*), which included a change of clothes (one of his tricks against the Minotaur was that he took with him two youngsters dressing them up as females). Participating in the feast were the *Deipnofores* (Δειπνοφόρες, *Dinner Bearers*), who pretended to be the mothers of the youths drawn by lot to be sent to the Minotaur. They brought them food and bread and told them stories in order to encourage and console them. The femininity of Theseus could be expressed in a positive way when he returned to the Athenian land where the presence of his father secured for him access to his own male gender.

A mother allows her boy to go to his father, to become a man. Based on her own sufficient paternal identifications, she leads her child into moving from the primary homosexuality with her on to the secondary one with his father. She frees her son form the fear of the pro-Oedipal woman.

When Theseus grew up and became strong enough, Aithra showed to him the rock which he had to lift in order to find underneath the sword and the sandals his father had hidden away for him. He had to take them back to his father, to be recognised by him as his legitimate heir.

Every son who is born a subject is assigned the struggle to liberate his mother from the supplication boughs of her own mother-ghosts that she brings to his nursery. Theseus was summoned by his mother to come (be born) to Eleusis as a liberating leader, to free her from the bondage of the supplication of the grieving mothers.

Eleusis (Ἐλευσίς) has the same etymological root as "coming" and "freedom" (*eleutheria*, ἐλευθερία). Coming of time? To be born, to take place. Eleutherai is called the site where the common soldiers were buried by Theseus.[2]

In *Suppliants* Theseus makes contact of identification with his mother, which helps him to tolerate patiently the gaps and contradictions of reality and transform them into uncertainties, ambiguities and paradoxes. Athenian politics provides a struggle for integration – and release from, rather than persecution by the shadows of supernatural elements of prehistory.

Of the supernatural forces and limits, feminine identification is the most difficult to assimilate. Euripides stages the feminine with division between male and female: the mother-daughter primary link and the move of the daughter towards the father.

The sacrifice

The sacrifice of Evadne occurs at the end of the tragedy, just before Athena appears to speak the truth that opens the future: Specific rituals need to be performed, sacrifice offered and oaths inscribed in order for the alliance between Athens and Argos to be binding.

At the end of the tragedy, Evadne performs a "marriage with death". She seems to be driven by an intense desire to unite with her husband in an eternal marriage that destroys the limits of reality. She wishes to be burned like her husband, who was torched by Zeus' lightning bolt. She appears mad from the anguish of her loss and passionate love. In the mania of her unbearable grief, and despite the pleas of her father Iphis, she leaps into the pyre to be united with her husband for eternity. There is no mention of Evadne's mother.

Is it her union with her primary mother that she desires? Is her suicide an ultimate effort to protect the secrecy and the sacredness of the self from the reality of the object that becomes immanent and poses a threat to its cohesion? We can't really know. There are mysterious links that are unknown to us. When we reach these early recesses (*mychoi, μύχοι*) of the house – self – where the mysterious leaps from body to psyche, from self to object, from unconscious to conscious take place – we are rendered "off subject". Only then can we become poetic, prophetic.

We feel that the tension is always somewhere else than in the place of its manifestation. Evadne puts an end to an unlocalisable loss by realising the wish of the mourners both to join their dead, and put them to death and separate from them. She opens the way for Athena to take her place and tell Athenians the truth about politics, and for the Epigonoi to undertake the future action.

Evadne presents her suicide as a sacrifice of the individual for the common good. She dies for her city, on behalf of all her mourning fellow citizens who are overwhelmed by devastating passions. She captures the fire and stems the flood of the mournful emotions in a single human act. She performs an act of mastery. She masters the madness of the epidemic and war that has invaded her. She wants to do it right. She presents her sacrifice as an act of war, as an active reaction to passive living. She voluntarily offers her body to be sacrificed for the sake of the community.

Evadne renounces her bonds with her father Iphis and her own sons. She discards the reality of time and surrenders to the flames or the pyre that represents the gift of passion and destruction, the eternal union, the loss of anticipation for the future and the memory of the past.

Wilkins (1990:181) examines Euripides' innovation in which "the sacrifice is transferred from the soldiers in the army to the literal but equally voluntary sacrifice of the individual – where the individual is usually a young woman" Foley (1985:39) argues that

> sacrificial procedure offers to the poet grammar of procedural terms by which to articulate in a compressed and symbolic form the nature of relations . . . between men in the community and of men to the larger world of animals and gods around them.

The Eleusinian promise

We can say that Evadne's self-immolation opens a window to the Eleusinian Mysteries. She throws herself into her husband's funeral pyre and arrives at the marriage chamber of Persephone. In Homeric Hymn to Demeter, Persephone leaves her husband Hades, ascends to the light of life and fertility and joyfully reunites with her mother Demeter. Evadne does the reverse, leaping down into the fire, leaving her desolate father Iphis behind. The critics comment on the vertical axis of Evadne's leap from the cliff to the pyre.

EVADNE: It's useless. You can't reach me, can't take my hand.
My body falls: whatever you suffer
My husband and I burn together.

Evadne in a way tells her father: My hand is not yours to give to another man. You can't give me away for a new marriage. You can't give me to time. It's useless. Words, reason, limits, time, father are useless. Evadne leaps into the flames behind the stage – skene. The Chorus and Iphis break into a dirge.

CHORUS: Woman, what horror
IPHIS: I am finished, daughters of Argos
CHORUS: To have lived through such savagery-
Can you bare to see what she dared?

[1021–1027]

This is a scene of rupture. What happens now is beyond words, beyond meaning and politics. Evadne is all alone now and beyond any reach. Like the dead, like a bird, she flies away. She wishes to live with – by dying with – her husband, that is, she desires to be united with her husband in death, in an endless love, free from any labour.

Evadne is either too high above or too far below her father, beyond contact. His hands cannot reach her. This is a negative image to that of Theseus joining hands with his mother, liberating her from the supplication when they leave Eleusis. Their departure for Athens' political places sustains the Eleusinian promise of parent-child reunion; the eternal separation of Iphis and Evadne shatters it. "Mirroring Demeter's journey to Eleusis in search of her lost daughter, Iphis knows nothing of the myth's restorative conclusion, or of the promise it offers to those initiated in its Mysteries" (Rhem, 2002:28).

In the place of the Eleusinian promise, politics work with negotiations. The male and female elements of the foundations of the polis are in constant negotiation between joining and refusing hands and between sustaining and shattering the Eleusinian promise of primary union, as the process of un-integration-integration-disintegration develops.

Kapaneus' heroism is mirrored in Evadne's devotion to her dead husband. In an analogous way the sons' devotion to their dead hero fathers (the offspring of lions, according to Athena) will lead them to risk their lives in a future war.

Exit from their trap, freedom, is a basic wish for a woman. From the top of her *airy rock* (*aitheria petra, αἰθερία πέτρα*) Evadne hangs in the air in a deadly upward swing (*aiorema, αἰώρημα*) above Capaneus' pyre, like a bird. It is as if the place below, whether on the ground or in the underworld, "could be reached only by first rising up". The bird is a powerful image that refers to a woman's wish to fly, to escape. Death is an escape. Women throw themselves into the air; they have a natural rapport with the beyond, like poets and prophets. While man, as a hoplite, has to hold his ground and face death head on, for an Athenian woman death means an exit. Evadne with a leap left her father's house to reach the rock from which she was to throw herself by another sudden leap to Hades (Loraux, 1987:18–19).

Loraux (1987:23–26) argues: A man dies by murder, while a woman by sacrifice. A woman escapes from life by suicide. Her sacrifice happens in the space where she belongs. The chamber of death is connected to the wedding thalamus, where femininity is legitimised. A woman in Ancient Athens does not belong to the polis, but to her husband. Marriage tolerates pleasure in the wedding thalamus – in the depth of the house – on the bed which above all is the place of procreation. Evadne goes to the extreme in order to fulfil the Eleusinian promise, thus showing the limits of politics.

Tension between harmony of union and differentiation of autonomy

Throughout the play we observe a tension between obtaining a fusion and harmony of union, on the one hand, and being a separate-differentiated autonomous tragic subject on the other. Being one with the world, nature, earth, mother, community, makes the fear of becoming free and autonomous tolerable.

Melting is a frequent word in the play, a powerful metaphor of abolishing every limit that separates and differentiates; melting in glowing fire, dying with, melting in the air, vanishing in the air, the body melting away without food, melting in desire, etc. This is an important force in the reality of a social group.

We can imagine that the "melting" is an image of the sense of being, primary union, lasting existence. Melting is also used to describe the abolishing of any limits of space while realising the wish for fusion. This is the beginning of the process of internalisation.

"Dying with" (*synthanein, συνθανείν*) is a wish often expressed in the play (by the grieving mothers, Adrastos and Evadne). It means the ultimate union between self and object. We can think that by her suicide, Evadne is united with her primary object in a fusion, reaching a state of undifferentiating. She perfectly blends Eros and Thanatos together and is freed to live eternally while in reality she dies.

Then there come the painful separation, differentiation and integration, the fear of integration, followed by the fear of being attacked from the outside; the struggle of life and the fear of a breakdown that follows a movement of integration.

When you deal with these primitive forces (which lie at the foundation of politics) you cannot inform yourself or the others by using reason and objective reporting. You need emotional experiences. You need art. Words that touch are those that bear the weight of affect and the unmoved rock of primitive experiences (Manolopoulos, 2015).

The disruptive otherness of the feminine

The poet of the world's grief (Hamilton, 1930) struggles with the use of his metaphors and ritual performances to link the mysterious supernatural forces and anachronistic mythic ideal to modern democracy, which is dominated by chance and incomprehensible forces. The modern polis struggles to integrate its attractive and threatening archaic forces. The *Suppliants* include the feminine as a disruptive otherness that threatens the cohesion of the polis.

"Recognition (*anagnorisis, ἀναγνώρισις*) of persons whose identities were unknown or mistaken is a typical and even focal device of tragic action. However, this literal type of recognition is the overtly theatrical event that condenses the epistemological bias of the entire phenomenon of drama. Thus, recognition extends embracing the world, the other, and the self. The problem of accurately reading the other is a continuing, obsessive concern in Greek tragedy that increases in urgency as a genre displays a greater self-consciousness with regard to its theatrical resources" (Zeitlin, 1996:362). Zeitlin argued that the patriarchic structure of society in Ancient Athens influenced all institutions of culture. In ancient tragedy we see women being used not as separate and autonomous subjects but as symbols, who are valuable only in facilitating and perpetuating male discourse. The question is how "playing the other" happens.

Mendelsohn (2002) refers to writers of the feminist movement, and reads in ancient tragedies the ways politics is shaped in striving to regulate the subversive unruly feminine nature. Women try to escape the tyrannical oppressive limitations of patriarchy and this subversive action is the source of conflict that shapes the political order in each society at the level of rules and laws of the state.

The female is understood as "unruly, sexually and emotionally excessive, wild; she must be tamed, domesticated, 'yoked.' " This understanding means that "the feminine is associated with the wild and the bestial, whereas the masculine is associated with civilisation and culture." A different interpretation is that tragedy's women appear "in order to problematise the ideologies that the mythic tradition had presumably been created to reinforce" (Mendelsohn, 2002:20).

A fire of madness

A fire of madness emerges in mothers of newborn babies. According to the Homeric Hymn to Demeter, the inconsolable goddess was wandering wanton and homeless throughout Greece, looking for her lost daughter. At Eleusis, she concealed her divine identity and became wet-nurse to Demophon, the newborn son of the king. In order to make him immortal, she fed him ambrosia during the day and at night she placed him in the flames of the hearth that are never extinguished to burn his mortal parts. The newborn's mother realised what was going on and terrified she interrupted the process. Irate Demeter disclosed that she was a goddess and accused the mortals of not being able to tell who is god and who is demon. The anonymous ghosts – unintegrated elements of unresolved mourning – visiting the nursery, require that the parents undertake them as subjects, give them a sufficient meaning and place them within time and reality. The aim is to prevent them from passing on to the next generation.

We hope that the mother holds her newborn infant with a capacity for reverie, moderation and an adequate ego and superego function that regulates her erotic and destructive flaming passions. Euripides' tragic figures pray that Aphrodite will not strike them in all her might, but in moderation. The wild beast, attributed to women, feared by men and women, comes from this early epoch of individual development, when the infant is at the mercy of the mother's pathos. The fire of the aggressive and erotic passions of women is depicted by Euripides in many of his tragedies.

We are passive towards a passion, we suffer it and this is terrifying. The passion is linked to nature and the feminine core of existence (Bell, 2007:9). Theseus is constantly locked in impassioned battles with feral, hybrid creatures and he appears as conqueror (by charm or violence) of women. The women he lay with had desires beyond the ordinary. In the amazon combat, barbarity is feminine and takes the place of the monstrous (Green, 1980).

Devereux (1981) cites Clement of Alexandria, who wrote about the "mysteries of Athenians", sung in Orpheus' poems. Baubo hosts the wandering Demeter and offers her wine and meal. The goddess declines it because she is in mourning. Baubo uncovered her genitals and exhibited them to her. Demeter spontaneously laughed, pleased at the spectacle and then received the wine. Baubo showed Demeter the site from where a newborn emerges. A new Kore will be conceived and born every year, mortal for the time she lives.

Mendelsohn (2002:20) observes that

> the inclusion of ostensibly incongruous feminine passions in *Suppliant Women*... was in fact a special Euripidean innovation – a self-conscious addition of the feminine to mythic narratives that (before) had . . . focused on the masculine, martial and "political".

Loraux (1987:30) proposes that ancient "tragedy constantly disturbs the norm in the interest of the deviant, but at the same time we must be aware that under the deviant the norm is silently present". Women are the actors of this silent psychic and social representation. The deviant forces that stray from normality are the ones ultimately affirming the order of politics.

The Greek drama employs the feminine as the tragic symbol for the forces ("diversity") that threaten the civic entity and its ideological structure ("unity"). The polis is by definition an entity that forms a unity and therefore it suppresses contradiction and diversity (Loraux, 1986).

Evadne echoes the unending woe which resounds from the laments of the chorus. A brief sudden dramatic turn of events, a coup de théâtre reverses and externalises the trauma of painful loss.

EVADNE: yes, I see my deliverance,
Fate keeps step with my dance.
For glory I'll cast myself
from this jut of cliff
and leap to the funeral pyre:
melting in radiant flame
my body will mingle with yours,
loved husband, flesh to flesh,
down in Persephone's house-
I'll never betray your death
by clinging to life on earth.
Sunlight, goodbye. Goodbye,
marriage. Not for me those

beds of virtuous
which bring
forth children to Argos.
My true wedded husband
Melts in a pure wind
With his life in a single fire

[965–983]

An essential paranoia linked to the feminine lies at the foundation of polis

There are various complementary interpretations of the paranoia that is inherent in an organization. Paranoia is a disturbance of linking and separating between internal (psychic) and external (social) reality, which is crucial in politics. The paranoid is afraid of the dissolution of any order and organisation, and wishes to have control over it. He attacks internal and external reality with denials and manic sadistic control, in order to dissolve the rock of historical truth. The paranoiac fear that the cohesion of the self and of the group will be dissolved results in the increase of control mechanisms to maintain unity.

The agony of disintegration is inherent in any social group. The word *"agony"* (ἀγωνία) in ancient Greek is linked etymologically to the word *"agon"* (ἀγών, debate, argument, game) which is derived from the verb *"ago"* (ἄγω, lead, direct, head, steer, give an aim).

When an individual is integrated, he faces the fear of integration. This is the fear that an attack will come from outside, and the organisation will be dissolved. Any integration entails an act of differentiation that establishes an identity. What are rejected returns threateningly to attack the self. A father is then needed to help the child overcome this acute paranoia with the aid of transitional objects that transform the contradictions to paradoxes used for playing. A leader is needed to help the city overcome the fear of integration with good politics.

Much of Euripides' use of argumentation depicts this human effort to buffer the acute paranoiac fear of attack when integration takes place. Athenian democracy struggles to balance public life oscillating between the fear of integration, constitutional equality of the members of the society, and the power of the leaders. There is a continuum between lack of adequate maternal mirroring, corruption of ethical values, paranoia, pathology of narcissism, lying culture, betrayal, and perverted exhibitionism. What makes someone behave like a traitor is fear of integration.

The paranoid rejects the primary identification; he does not integrate his femininity; he does not know if he is a man or a woman, he is depersonalised and puts a neo-reality of delusion in the place of lacking or inadequate primary identifications. There is a parallel between the delusional neo-reality of the paranoid and, other things been equal, the paranoiac relationship between a daughter and her mother (Green, 1972:207). Green cites the story of Herakles who in a fit of madness murdered his friend Iphitos, and thus was punished to be a slave for three years to Omphale, queen of Lydia. He became her lover but while in her service he was transformed into an effeminate man, dressed as a woman spinning the wheel, virile yet harmless. The etymological root of Omphale is the word "navel" (*omphalos, ὀμφαλός*).

Encysted in the foundations of the polis is madness, an inherent paranoia caused by failure of the maternal holding, which results in the rejection of primary identification. What is encysted may erupt with violence in incomprehensible events. The attacks on the primary maternal identifications connect femininity, paranoia and politics with the need to control and to communicate (Green, 1972).

The compulsive need of men and women to communicate and exhibit themselves shamelessly in public can be thought as a self-healing defence. It is related to the essential need to find in social reality what they lack in their psychic world: an internalised object that can adequately mirror and reliably respond and return the confirmation of their investment.

The role of mother fixation in paranoia is observed in the *Suppliants* in men and women. Evadnes' episode causes a sense of depersonalisation, a state where the links of primary and secondary identifications are broken. At the same time, Evadne offers her body to bridge the gap of depersonalisation, the painful experience of loss that reaches and mobilises deep split-off elements (internal-external reality, male-female, dead-alive object). Her episode is a dramatic example of neo-reality. This "drama within the drama" (Zuntz, 1955), like a dream within a dream, is the return of the split off unbearable trauma and its encysted madness. This is followed by Athena's call for negotiation.

Mendelsohn (2002:233–234) concludes: The oscillation between competing models and the explosion of opposite types and genres is the poet's way of positing a tentative middle ground. This pattern argues against a dismissal of the poet and his work as patriarchal. "Oscillation, conflict, equilibrium, negotiation" provides Euripides' political plays with their subject matter, and their very structure. Only after we have understood that the *Suppliant Women* is constructed as a living theatrical example of the complex principle of negotiation, can we see it as a coherent and especially dramatic art investigation into the nature of the democratic polis, in other words as a truly political play.

Two deities representing almost irreconcilable aspects of the world

Two deities, representing irreconcilable aspects of the world, preside over the play. One is Demeter, the goddess of fertility, marriage, and the cycle of life, death, and rebirth; the other is Athena, the goddess of wisdom, political discourse, and military action.

> The two framing deities, present only at the beginning and the end of the play, set as foreground the world of human activity and individual tragedy against a wider background; the context of genetic and universal forces (or divine beings personifying those universals.
>
> (Scully, 1995:4–5)

Demeter is the mother of Kore, whose loss drove her into deep mourning. Eleusis is the place of her cult, a mother goddess and her daughter. The mother-daughter relationship keeps the rhythm to the life-death cycle and back to life again. Kore is lost and returns to earth every year. New crops and new corpses come and go from and to the earth in the *Suppliant Women* (Storey, 2008:18).

Demeter, the holder of Eleusinian land, symbolises earth (mother), and ghearth (Hestia). Athena is not born by a woman, has nothing to do with feminine matter, mother-daughter loss, mourning and melancholy. Athena demands blood vengeance. Demeter represents the supernatural forces of femininity, fertility, primary identification. She represents what Winnicott calls the "being". Athena represents the "doing", which Winnicott (1971:72–85) assigns to instinctual drives. Athena is not like a mother and nothing like a daughter. She never faced the dilemma of how to leave the mother and move towards a new different object, the father. She was born of her father's intelligence. Athena is the necessary compliment to Demeter who bears the pacific spirit.

At the start, Demeter's place is taken by Aithra on the ground of the orchestra. Aithra from the opening of the play is placed in sharp contrast between worshippers and mourners and feels the tension between the burial rite that is unfulfilled and the fertility rite that is interrupted. In the end, Athena takes the place of Evadne, standing high above the stage. "The split focus – immortal on high, mortals below – simultaneously acknowledges and denies the lessons about violent excess that the play has exposed" (Rhem, 2002:31). In the foundation of the polis lie forces of splitting, i.e. simultaneous recognition and denial of reality.

The sanctuary of Eleusis and the agora of Athens, Demeter, and Athena, are two aspects of the polis. Demeter links us with mourning and femininity;

her mystery is Panhellenic and offers communal experience of light and hope, bridging the gap between death and immortality. Athena, the goddess of Athens, offers boundaries of institutions and frames of separations that are foundations of civilisation.

Politics lies in a space of struggle between these two irreconcilable goddesses, two aspects of the identity of the polis. The conflict between male and female elements of experience is inherent in the foundations of the democratic polis. The constant negotiation that we observe in the Suppliants does not aim at resolving the conflict between paternal and maternal identifications that constitute psychic bisexuality.

Since the beginning of life there has been tension between elements of limiting experiences and elements of receiving experiences, which respectively form the foundations of male and female identifications, ultimately constructing psychic bisexuality. The aim is to maintain the tension between these elements from which conflict and creative solutions are generated.

Law is rooted in the magic curse

During the three-day feast of Thesmoforia (*Θεσμοφόρια*) the assembly and the courts ceased functioning and the prisoners were liberated. The laws were in search of their primitive magical roots.

Harrison (1903) wrote about Thesmoforia (Θεσμοφόρια), the most ancient and foremost feast of cleansing: It was performed by married women in the sowing season. The mythological explanation was that the feast of the abduction of the Kore by Hades was being celebrated. Falling into the opening chasm in the earth beside the Kore were also the pigs that happened to feed there at the time.

The Thesmoforoi threw into the fissures of Demeter also newborn piglets. The chasms were fissures in the earth or artificial crypts, sites for rituals that had been converted into temples of earthly divinities. The piglets had to stay enough time in the earth to rot. Inside the chasms there were snakes, the guardians of the sanctuaries that devoured the greatest part. Snake and male organ effigies were also made of thick wheat pulp, which were thrown into the sanctuaries together with fir cones and the pigs. These sacra were magic potions of fertility.

Some of the women purified themselves for three days and on the first day, that of Descent and Ascent, they descended to the inner sanctum, placed the piglets to rot and recovered the remnants of the decayed flesh left there the previous year, bringing them up again to lay on the altars. Whoever took a piece of them and mixed it with the seeds he would sow was certain to have a good harvest. The second day was one of austere Fasting. The women would place the magic sacra on the altars and then sit on the ground and indulge in obscene language. They then got up and feasted, imitating the powerful onset of spring. On the third day, named Good Birth (*Kalligeneia, Καλλιγένεια*), they sacrificed and ate meat. Finally, they sowed the rotten flesh in the fields.

The logical explanation is that the mysteries were called Thesmoforia because it was the feast of Demeter Thesmoforos, the one who introduced institutions, agriculture, house life, marriage, etc. *Thesmoi* (*Θεσμοί*) means Laws in Greek. Thesmoforos Demeter was considered a Law Giver.[3] Harrison prefers a different explanation: The pigs and other sacra ended up being "thesmoi", a noun derived from the verb "thetein" (*θέτειν*) which means to place down, therefore they were "objects laid down". The women were called Thesmoforoi because they carried or bore the "objects to be laid down" – the verb *fero* (*φέρω*) meaning to bear, carry. What are the objects that are laid down? The word law has its roots in magic, which bears the curse and was transformed into a religious oath and prayer (wish) and social convention and law.

In a basic substratum of primary aloneness and intimacy, a primordial matrix of intersubjectivity, undifferentiated traces of the self and the object are inscribed. They are deposited initially into the mother (our first legislator), then the family and finally they are laid down in the settings of our institutions (stable relationships based on a contract). The settings of our reliable institutions (stable relationships based on a contract) absorb these highly subjective and undifferentiated elements, so that within the bounds, we feel secure. In these frames we have "deposited" our immortality. Without the frames, we would not have a place of jurisdiction as competent subjects who are present to live and think their experiences (Freud', 1937b; Bleger, 1967; Bion, 1962; Tustin, 1986; Winnicott, 1988; Kristeva, 2000).

We can now associate the Mysteries with the horror we feel when we are confronted suddenly with an uncanny experience (Freud, 1919). Eleusis is the place where death and birth alternate. Here, Euripides casts birth, death and war together, which suddenly bring forth the unfamiliar, what is outside the hearth of the house, outside the subject, and the safety of the stable frames. The uncanny threatens the boundaries of the self and so it makes them acutely perceived.

The needs of the ego for dependence on the object, make the individuals become subjects, come out of their selves and find-create a polis where they can address their supplications in order to be heard and be responded to. However, the settings of the polis' institutions are constantly disturbed, narcissistic integrity is overturned and the undifferentiated traces of experience are liberated and at large, available elaboration and integration. Then new events are created, new forms of sociality and galaxies of subjectivity.

The functional, transparent, and permeable framework of an institution allows new events to happen. When the frames are based on rigid splits their rift releases split-off elements with pain, grief and violent explosions. The frames then become hardened, overdetermined, and over construed. Then nothing happens. The frames are saturated with meanings, typified speech, fakery, under the fear of breakdown. The underlying agony of annihilation is unthinkable (Winnicott, 1974:106).

Freud (1939:74–76) discovered that split off traces of preverbal traumas are taken up in character formations and return in demonic repetitions of everyday transferences. Traumas are also taken up in institutions (social "character" formations) which have anti-traumatic functions. Ego needs of dependence create the subject and institute the polis. The subjects and the polis need to defend their integrity either with the positive narcissism of life or the negative narcissism of death (internal or external mafia-like organisations) (Rosenfeld, 1971:174).

We become subjects within the city, not in isolation. In feasts, ceremonies, assemblies we waver. Through mythical thought we create the self-illusion of the "holy" unity of the polis. We imagine the polis as another subject that listens and makes reply to us (Freud, 1921; Bion, 1961). An institution is not a thinking subject. It is a "character" that functions with the aim of perpetuating its organisation. It is an anti-tragic "machine" where resides the demon of repetition. We, the subjects of a democratic polis, transform this "machine" to a "Deus ex Machina", which listens and responds, and gives to the plot coherence and an outcome, with the poetic conviction of a hallucinatory realisation.

We, the subjects, give to our polis the sense of the tragic. It is us who have intent and guilt, not the institution. We regress, we speak again the secret language of preverbal "feelings", we find the mother-environment again who listens; we do not talk in the desert, we become authors, collectors of stray thoughts, we think about them giving them a home, a story, a place to place the self.

Birth and war

The Suppliants are mothers. They ask why they should give birth to children; to send them off to be killed in a war. Birth-giving is a battle both for the baby and the mother. Men become women as the pain of the wounded soldier is likened to the pain of labour.[4]

> In a wondrously gender-confounding moment, war blurs the distinction of the sexes in relation to the very acts – battle, childbirth – normally seen as their most representative and distinctive of roles. It reduces

dying men to the state of women as the bearers of new life, while also giving to both of them the right to be named for posterity on their tombs.
(Rose, 2018:47–50)

The expectant mother does not deny violence. She dreams of violent deaths, projecting to the father the violence away from the baby she carries in her womb. She feels hatred, love, and erotic arousal towards the newborn. Her hatred sets a limit the infant knocks against in trying to identify itself as a separate subject. Sentimentality is useless for a mother (Winnicott, 1947; Rose, 2018:114).

We can think of politics in a democratic polis as the prototype of maternal care – infant unit; the position of the Suppliant mothers is not a denial of hate and separation. It is not an exploitation of emotions and a waste of objects. It is a tragic political position of integrating one's impulses, trusting that the object will survive, making the object to be separate and useful, and the self a subject who has the capacity to use the object (Winnicott, 1971).

The object becomes objective, it acquires full rights of existence (meaning, autonomy, and integration). It is rescued from the shadows of semi-existence, the uncanny ghosts of the traumatically lost but unmourned objects and the not yet born (unsymbolised and undifferentiated) ones.

Psychoanalysis investigates how the demonic compulsion to repeat (character) is related to the thought (subject) and how the exciting relationship to the subjective object is transformed to the capacity to use the objective object. We explore how the subject makes the trauma a personal experience for the repetition and meaningful reflection of which is itself responsible (Winnicott, 1960:37, 1971). How does the subject place himself under the regime of meaning making and internalization processes? How does he achieve the sense of the tragic?

Dictators cannot make a tragedy. They create melodramas in their effort not to help us communicate and think but to make us feel moved. They ask the polis to cry for them. They ask us not only to fear but also to love them. We cannot place them outside our omnipotence. They do not survive as objects outside our omnipotence that saves them. They either collapse or take revenge. They waste our transference investments, soon becoming useless as objects. They state their immortality not in the frames of institutions – they haven't got that far yet – but in the pre-Oedipal mother with which they identify (Winnicott, 1950:253). Nikjolai Rimsky-Korsakov wrote the liberto of his opera Kashchey the Deatless, based on the story of one of the most famous heroes of Russian fairy tales. The demonic evil, tyrannical wizard, who menaced yound women, cannot die, because he has hidden his death in one of his daughters tears. The cruel daughter has frozen her emotions, she cannot cry. When finally she falls in love, reaches her Oedipus complex, loses her beloved prince to a rival princes, then she can cry and free her father, letting him die.

Benjamin (1925:103) stated that the demonic is linked to the tragic in the same way that ambiguity is to paradoxical. We can think that politics ina a democratic Polis is the struggle of the work of culture to hold a transitional space of playing where we transform the ambiguities of the demonic repetitions into contradictions of paradoxes that we can tolerate with a sense of tragic. Freedom is identical with the capability for a new start. A dictator is afraid of and loathes making new starts. He stops the flow of time, the process of succession. Every newborn child is a supreme moment against totalitarianism (Arendt, 1979; Rich, 1986; Rose, 2018:79). In contrast, Euripides, like a child, loves surprises, the future. He loves the origins, and the beginnings.

Notes

1 Another hypothesis is that the word mystery comes from the word *mysos* (μύσος), which means *miasma* and evokes the idea that what is hidden inside the body is evil and needs cleansing with a sacrifice which is all what religions is about (Harrison, 1903).
2 This site was a village on the border between Attica and Boiotia. The inhabitants of Eleutherai had freely chosen to be Athenian citizens. They worshipped Dionysos Eleuthereus, the patron god of the City Dionysia.
3 A. Freud (1965:168) described the mother as the first external legislator for her infant.
4 In a version of Theseus' myth, Ariadne dies at childbirth in Amathous, Cyprus, taking Theseus' baby to the grave with her. Theseus established a ritual at Amathous whereby a young person lay down and mimicked the screams and gesticulations of women in labour.

References

Arendt H. (1979) *The Origins of Totalitarianism*. New York: Harcourt Brace Jovanovich.

Bell D. (2007) Psychoanalytic Perspectives on the Dionysiac and the Apollonian in Euripides's Bacchae. In C. Bainbridge, et al. (Eds.) *Culture and the Unconscious*. Basingstoke UK, Palgrave MacMillan.

Benjamin W. (1925) *The Origins of German Tragic Drama*, trans. J. Osborne. New York: Verso, 1998.

Bion W. (1961) *Experiences in Groups and Other Papers*. London, Tavistock.

———. (1962 [1984]) *Learning from Experience*. London, Karnac Books.

———. (1965 [1984]) *Transformations*. London, Karnac Books.

Bleger J. (1967 [2013]) *Symbiosis and Ambiguity: A Psychoanalytic Study*. London, Routledge.

Chabert C. (2019) Plural Feminine: Hysteria, Masochism or Melancholia? *International Journal of Psycho-Analysis*, *100*(3), 584–592.

Denis P. (1982 [2010]) Primary Homosexuality: A Foundation of Contradictions. In D. Briksted-Breen, S. Flandres and A. Gibeault (Eds.) *Reading French Psychoanalysis*. London and New York, Routledge.

Devereux G. (1981) *Baubo, la vulve mythique*. Paris, Payot. In Greek. Athens, Olkos (1997).

Euripides'. (1995) *Suppliant Women*. (Trans. R. Warren and S. Scully). Oxford, Oxford University Press.

Foley P. H. (1985) *Ritual Irony: Poetry and Sacrifice in Euripides*. Ithaca and London, Cornell University Press.

Foley P. H. (1994) *The Homeric Hymn to Demeter: Translation, Commentary, and Interpretative Essays*. Princeton, Princeton University Press.

Freud A. (1965) *Normality and Pathology in Childhood: Assessments of Development*. New York, International Universities Press.

Freud S. (1895 [1950]) Project for a Scientific Psychology. *S.E.*, *1*.

———. (1913) The Theme of Three Caskets. *S.E.*, *13*.

———. (1919) The Uncanny. *S.E.*, *17*.

———. (1921) Group Psychology and the Analysis of the Ego. *S.E.*, *18*.

———. (1937a) Analysis Terminable and Interminable. *S.E.*, *23*.

———. (1937b) Constructions in Analysis. *S.E.*, *23*.

———. (1939) Moses and Monotheism. *S.E.*, *23*.

Green A. (1972) Aggression, Femininity, Paranoia and Reality. *International Journal of Psycho-Analysis*, *53*, 205–211.

———. (1980) Thésée et Oedipe. Une iterprétation psychanalytique de la Théséide. In *Psychanalyse et Culture Greque. Confluents Psychanalytique*. Paris, Les Belles Lettres. In Greek (Trans. M. Fragopoulos). Athens, Rappa (1985).

Hamilton E. (1930 [2017]) *The Greek Way*. New York, W.W. Norton & Company.

Harrison J. (1903 [1992]) *Prolegomena to the Study of Greek Religion*. Princenton, NJ, Princeton University Press. In Greek (Trans. E. Papadopoulou). Athens, Iamvlihos (1996).

Kristeva J. (2000 [2007]) From Symbols to Flesh: The Polymorphous Destiny of Narration. In P. Williams and G. Gabbard (Eds.) *Key Papers in Literature and Psychoanalysis*. London, Karnac Books.

Loraux N. (1986) *The Invention of Athens: The Funeral Oration in the Classical City*. Cambridge, MA, Harvard University Press.

———. (1987) *Tragic Ways of Killing a Woman*. Cambridge MA, Harvard Universities Press.

Manolopoulos S. (2015) Medea by Euripides: Psychic Constructions for Preverbal Experiences and Traumas. *The Psychoanalytic Quarterly*, *84*(2), 441–461.

March J. (1990) Euripides the Misogynist? In A. Powel (Ed.) *Euripides, Women and Sexuality*. London and New York, Routledge.

Mendelsohn D. (2002) *Gender and the City in Euripides' Political Plays*. New York, Oxford University Press.

Petrou A. (2019) Mother's Primacy in Anthropology and Psychoanalysis. *Romanian Journal of Psychoanalysis*, *12*(2), 70–92.

Plutarch's. (1993) *Lives, Theseus and Romulus, Lycurgus and Numa, Solon and Publicola*. (Trans. B. Perrin). Cambridge, MA, Harvard University Press.

Potamianou A. (1996) *Hope: A Shield in the Economy of Borderline States*. London and New York, Routledge.

Rhem R. (2002) *The Play of Space: Spatial Transformation in Greek Tragedy*. Princeton and Oxford, Princeton Universities Press.

Rich A. (1986 [1995]) *Of Woman Born: Motherhood as Experience and Institution*. New York, Norton.

Rose J. (2018) *Mothers: An Essay on Love and Cruelty*. London, Faber & Faber.

Rosenfeld H. (1971) A Clinical Approach to the Psychoanalytic Theory of the Life and Death Instincts: An Investigation into the Aggressive Aspects of Narcissism. *International Journal of Psycho-Analysis*, *52*, 169–178.

Scully S. (1995) Introduction. In *Euripides, Suppliant Women*. (Trans. Rosanna Warren and Stephen Scully). Oxford, Oxford University Press.

Storey C. (2008) *Euripides: Suppliant Women*. London, Duckworth.

Tustin F. (1986) *Autistic Barriers in Neurotic Patients*. London, Karnac Books.

Wilkins J. (1990) The State and the Individual: Euripides' Plays of Voluntary Self-Sacrifice. In A. Powel (Ed.) *Euripides, Women and Sexuality*. London and New York, Routledge.

Winnicott D. (1947 [1992]) *Hate in Countertransference: Through Paediatrics to Psycho-Analysis*. London, Karnac Books.

———. (1950 [1980]) Some Thoughts on the Meaning of the Word 'Democracy'. In *Home Is Where We Start From: Essays by a Psychoanalyst*. New York, Penguin Books.

———. (1960 [1990]) The Theory of Parent-Infant Relationship. In *The Maturational Processes and the Facilitating Environment*. London, Karnac Books.

———. (1965 [1990]) Communicating and Not Communication Leading to a Study of Certain Opposites. In *The Maturational Processes and the Facilitating Environment*. London, Karnac Books.

———. (1971) *Playing and Reality*. London, Tavistock.

———. (1974) The Fear of Breakdown. *International Review of Psychoanalysis*, *1*, 103–107.

———. (1988) *Human Nature*. London, Free Association Books.

Zeitlin F. (1996) *Playing the Other: Gender and Society in Classical Greek Literature*. Chicago and London, The University of Chicago Press.

Zuntz G. (1955) *The Political Plays of Euripides*. Manchester, Manchester University Press.

5   The order of politics

Sotiris Manolopoulos

The *Suppliants* ends with political negotiations, based on verbal language and sealed with mythical and religious beliefs, acts and oaths. People institute creative spaces of innovation and meeting places, where links of meaning are weaved and trading with substitute objects takes place; they use words and actions that tame reality, transforming it. Politics in a moderate democratic polis depends on the rule of law. It is based on – does not replace – mythical and religious beliefs and institutions. It consists in establishing alliances of community, which cannot be broken without "incalculable peril" to the polis and its people. It keeps in its core the early ethics of the infant – mother relationship where the links between them were inscribed in traces of memory standing against death.

Euripides does not bring resolutions. The unresolved, unfinished parts of the past are the cause of continuation in the future. They are also the cause of a fear that their return might bring chaos. The fear of dissolution haunts the polis all the time. A polis consists of contradictory split off uncompromising elements. Negotiation is the key word.

In the end Athena completes the play with clear instructions. The play presents mourning and femininity as elements of political negotiation between contradictory elements of experience. Through these negotiations, the contradictions and the ruptures of deep splits become hesitations, ambiguities, uncertainties, and paradoxes of a transitional space of the play.

In Euripides' *Suppliant Women* the political negotiations are linked to maternal persuasion. Euripides brings together the myth of the "male quest" embodied in the myths of Oedipus's sons and the female quest as it is represented in the Hymn to Demeter. "The poem's cyclical rather than linear narrative (mother and daughter separate and unite eternally in a seasonal pattern) represents a female quest" (Foley, 1994:xiii). Women founded the Eleusinian Mysteries; they know how the story ends; they write it. Reality becomes real through mourning and symbolisation. Words of persuasion are

DOI: 10.4324/9781003252184-6

mysterious passages; they separate and link body and psyche, life and death, pain and pleasure, fantasy and reality.

Uncertainties, ambiguities, and paradoxes substitute for agonies of annihilation, impasses, and contradictions

Euripides ironically introduces uncertainty into the myth. Uncertainty, ambiguity and paradoxes are introduced in the play as substitutes for agonies of annihilation and impasses of contradiction that occur when the subject is in transition, in a boundary, a third reality between being in union with the object and moving away to be integrated as separate and autonomous.

When the young generals, full of desire for glory, pressed Adrastos to launch the war against Thebes, they should have been protected from their omnipotence. This is what the omens said. King Adrastos should have said no to the disastrous expedition. Instead, he gave in to the extreme ambition of the young. This was a failure of politics; it was hubris. He betrayed the Eleusinian promise the leader gives to the polis and its subjects, to safeguard their sense of immortality.

The play starts with the destruction of the Argives' army because it denied the existence of supernatural forces beyond their arrogant omnipotence. The play ends with the acknowledgement of the divine powers that are expressed and bound in rites and rituals. The oaths of pacts should be inscribed, written. They are reminders of the written laws that bind the modern democratic polis.

Politics should listen to the mystical reading of omens. The seer that interprets the omens, the poet, informs politics. Religion continues in the transitional phenomena and objects of art. The Athenians have constructed an agora, as a make-believe transitional space for the special art of politics. There they can create, live, and share experiences and learn from them. They have founded this space on the belief that they are indigenous, immortal, and invincible. At the same time, their poet lets them know that there always is a negative aspect in their psychic and social constructions. Reality can intrude and overwhelm their political space in a harsh way, leaving the subjects feeling stripped, devoid of meaning.

Scully (1995:17–18) concludes: "This is a play of apparent resolutions and deep irresolution". Athena's epiphany [1135] is crucial for the content and the plot of the drama. Athena, neutral and indifferent to human feelings, reminds us of the harsh laws of political reality. Athena does not believe in reason and verbal promises of gratitude. She demands an alliance with Argos anchored in sworn oaths, sacrificial blood and sacred relics. She instructs Theseus to involve divine witnesses and physical reminders by means of a tripod, engraved written words and inscribed memory. Athena bestows a divine form upon the grim and uncompromising splits of reality of civic order, politics, and war.

The sworn oaths, sacrificial blood, and sacred relics, like the transitional phenomena, do not offer solutions by compromise but contain the contradictions and transform them into paradoxes of co-existence. The collective fantasies of our myths give coherence to our institutions and establish their origins. What in a culture is considered negative may be present in myths, rites, feasts, etc.

Negation (Freud, 1925) is used by civilisation. With the help of the symbol of negation, indispensable material for public life is released. The concepts of negation, splitting, and denial help us think of the external reality. The protective quality of negation enables us deal with a painful reality. It is an ally allowing for co-existence between the unacceptable and the realistic; it helps a polis forge its alliances. However, for the sake of psychic survival, negation may become radical splitting and extreme denial, which attack the subject's sense of reality and capacity to think, speak, and act. They remove the subject so that none are present, competent, and responsible, to live the experience, give it meaning, and integrate it.

Suppliant Women is a play of recognising and dealing with uncompromising, split-off elements, without seductive words covering the violent painful affects. The subjects use splitting and denial to calm down the agony. Politics is then presented as the art of holding, and employing transitional phenomena in public life with which the unbearable traumatic realities of annihilation are transformed into fears of breakdown, the splitting into demonic repetitions, the unbridgeable contradictions and impasses become paradoxes that can be tolerated and negotiated.

Boundaries: zones of shared reality

Politics in a democratic polis is subjected to the sense of the tragic. It aims at transforming the impossible impasses into a transitional spaces. It is the art of placing limits. It is part of the third reality, an intermediate zone between internal and external reality that enables us to bear the shock of the loss of omnipotence. Reality is a triadic phenomenon from the point of view of the subject who emerges, participates, observes, and thinks about it. This is the true self, who perceives creatively, in contrast to the false self who complies mechanically with reality.

We can think of boundaries as zones of shared reality, intermediate areas of transitional phenomena where we struggle to keep internal and external reality separate and linked. Our negative capabilities help us tolerate contradictions and transform them into uncertainties, ambiguities and paradoxes.

They help us invent innovative institutions, spaces of creativity to play with reality (French et al., 2009).

In these zones we meet with others and form alliances with them. There we struggle with irreducible splits inside psychic and social reality. These ruptures make it impossible to complete experiences and transform reality. They keep at work the fantasies of omnipotence, which render government, education, and psychoanalysis impossible professions.

In order to serve our interests, we seek and invest new aspects of the objects, we learn to understand what is good for us and how to take it in, what is bad and how to reject it, and we always negotiate, make exchanges, trade, and conclude agreements. The processes of mourning move between fantasy and reality and lead to a trade with a substitute object. With each step of representation, internalisation, and differentiation, new links are forged increasing the capacity of the network of exchanges (internal, external). A clear focus on the exchanges, which will benefit everyone – people and polis – is achieved. Agreements are made on the basis of clear exchanges.

In Sophocles' *Philoctetes*, Odysseus' skilful mediation was required to take the wounded and the deserted hero's invincible weapon, Herakles' bow and arrow that would help the Greeks win the war in Troy. A merchant unexpectedly appears on the scene signifying, I think, the arts of commerce, trade, and exchange as antidotes for war and therapy for the hero's isolation due to disease. Exchanges with allies and trade signify the end of wars and epidemics.

Exchanges with allies as the best antidote to war and commerce as therapy for social isolation were explored many centuries later by Claude Lévi-Strauss in *Tristes Tropiques* (1922). The networks of trade hold together contradictory elements and form a coherent functional whole. They require a sense of trust between people.

However, this trust can be betrayed, and the transitional objects and phenomena can be perverted. The hubristic people and the leader can collude and defend against the loss of omnipotence by manipulating the boundaries, corrupting the zones of the shared reality.

The *Suppliant Women* becomes a tragedy of knowledge and its negative (Storey, 2008:79, 92). The negative is constantly present as an achievement and casts a ray of hope for learning through experience. The play is a process of negotiating and sharing the power of politics and employing transitional phenomena in the place of omnipotence and the pathological negative of politics. Power can be shared, omnipotence cannot.

Rhem (2002:30–31) writes: The hubris of the Argive invasion "left its mark on Greek iconography in the depiction of Capaneus' omnipotence struck down by Zeus' lightning bolt as he mounds a siege ladder on the walls of Thebes". In contrast, Theseus, the democratic leader, struggles to restrain the violent destructive forces and he shows moderation, a power that can be shared.

The Athenians defend the rule of law; yet they recognise that the negative exists, the hubris of Argos and Thebes (the negative of Athens)

The *Suppliants* is the epitome of advocacy for political laws. Without the rule of law there would be no cohesion within the city based on freedom of the subject to think, speak and act in public life.

Theseus is given by the Suppliants as a prototype of the subject being in the public domain. Theseus "struggles" during the tragedy; he is open to external reality, he learns from experience, and he "turns around" (Dimakopoulou, 2014).

At the beginning, Theseus is certain that there is a clear-cut line between right and wrong that can be known, and the knowledge of the right can be acted upon. After he "wins victory in battle, successive waves of lament, eulogy, and desire for revenge will submerge the distinctions. . . . Personal emotion spills over into political signification" (Burian, 1985:138).

The *Suppliants* has been interpreted as representing the struggle of the Athenians to implement laws replacing mythical and religious beliefs and maintaining a moderate democracy, based on acknowledging individual responsibility for actions and beliefs, obeying the rule of law based on reason and words, and on forming alliances through compromise, reciprocity, mutual benefit, and harmony of peace.

We can think that what Euripides wants to appreciate is the need for theatrical poetic metaphors, mythical and religious acts, oaths and inscriptions of laws used in politics in order to help us tolerate the contradictions of split-off, untranslated impossible links (enigmas, according to Aristotle's Poetics) and transform them into uncertainties, ambiguities, and finally paradoxes.

Thebes is the negative of Athens. It is a despotic un-free state. Argos is the other negative of Athens, also a source of identification: a reckless, unfinished, unorganised state, on the brink of collapse, but not beyond repair. Finally, Adrastos is presented as a negative Theseus. He does not change during the play (Storey, 2008). He believes that we should go through life easily, without labours. He learns too late that no good fortune lasts for ever in the life of mortals.

Theseus, like Oedipus, becomes the legitimate leader when he discovers who he is, the murderer of his father, and integrates (becomes the subject of) his guilt. Not all leaders reach the Oedipal situation and internalise their guilt. Adrastos performed hubris in order to be punished from outside.

Euripides presented at the last moment a startling fact, which he introduced in the myth. Adrastos remembers that he – like Creon – remained silent when he was offered peace by Eteokles the last moment before he led his army to total destruction. He realises, too late, that he has brought this catastrophe upon himself and his fellow citizens; he is the subject responsible for his fate. The scholars observe: Zeus rules. The price for hubris is paid, first by Argos, now by Thebes – and by Athens soon? We should ponder on it even at this very last moment.

The Herald makes important criticism regarding the role of demagogues and the unwillingness of simple people to allow for time to think out the issues, following instead whoever is persuasive. Theseus says: Here is a clever Herald. The Herald sounds contemporary in his criticism against democracy. Not everything he (the Herald) says can be dismissed simply as "idle words" "The acrimonious stichomythia with which the agon ends, displays a number of the specifically political themes of the play. . . . The contest of words is at an end and there is no choice but to fight" (Burian, 1985:142–143).

There is a limit to how much a democracy can process politically. There is a limit to how much the psychic work can elaborate before it fails.

The fear of extinction

In the *Suppliants*, Euripides projects horrific images: Capaneus who is burnt by Zeus's thunderbolt; Amphiaraus who, along with his chariot, is swallowed up by the earth falling in a chasm (split); the bloody battle scenes of Theseus and his Athenians before the walls of Thebes; Evadne throwing herself in the pyre. Faced with the horror of the abyss with no response from the object, the subject creates horrific demonic images in order to fill it.

The imposition of silence stems from a primitive nameless dread (Bion, 1962). The chorus of the grieving mothers remains on stage throughout the drama, but most of the time they bear silently their pain; politics is in action. Also, their grandsons stay silent until before the end of the play when they continue the chorus' lament and promise to continue the war.

We expect Athens to feel the fear of annihilation during a war. This is the fear that its civilisation has no future; it will be destroyed. Without a sense of the future (the succession by the next generation, which gives the polis the sense of immortality), a community is paralysed by the anxiety of becoming extinct. Without the sense of immortality, a community will be paralysed by the agony of annihilation and protective omnipotent fantasies of fusion with apathy, immobility, and despair as a result (Nociforo, 2017). It may seek refuge in the eternal repetitions of actions and omnipotent fantasies of merging, resulting in superficial harmony, stifling rigidity, apathy, indifference, and immobility.

The agonies of annihilation derive from early failures of integration of space and time. These agonies regarding the integration of space and time are mobilised par excellence in politics. There is always an underlying fear that the integrity of the polis will be dissolved. Is this why Athens went to war, to keep her coherence?

In Euripides' *Suppliants*, the omnipresent Demeter, the goddess of harvest, reminds us that in an agricultural society, the fears of a crop failure activate agonies of annihilation and infantile experiences of biological helplessness. The polis and its subjects, the political animals, are phenomena of nature and culture; they produce politics, a transitional reality, in order to face the experiences of helplessness.

Between the "stateless" state and tyranny, a democratic polis

Between the unorganised, "stateless" state and the tyranny of autarchy there is the democratic state that strives through politics to keep the processes of transformation open-ended, in transition. The moment of transition is the most tragic in any development.

There is a "narrow corridor" between the need to have a strong state, which is not despotic, and a free state which is not "stateless", disorderly. The strong state is a shackled state, bound by institutions, guiding principles, and the laws, through which the society controls the state. When the new alphabet was invented (borrowed from the Phoenicians) the laws began to be written down in ancient Athens; the creation of the city state started in 621 BC by Dracon and was completed less than 30 years later by Solon. The city was then able to begin its democratic evolution.

It is accountable to society . . . because it is shackled by people who will complain, demonstrate, and even rise up if it oversteps its limits. Its presidents and legislators are elected, and they are kicked out of office when the society they are ruling over doesn't like what they are doing. Its bureaucrats are subject to review and oversight. It is powerful, but coexists with and listens to a society that is vigilant and willing to get involved in politics and contest power.

(Acemoglu and Robinson, 2020:27).

The first legislator is an external divine power, the mother. A. Freud (1965:173) observes that the gap between internal and external laws narrows as the individual's maturation deepens. This is the narrow corridor of democracy.

Cartledge (2009:2, 62, 68) paraphrasing a quotation from Shelley, he says that that early Greek poets from Homer to Pindar were the "acknowledged legislators of the world". Solon combined poetry and politics in a practical way. Also, tragic poets presented a medium for thinking and practising politics. They acknowledged the creative potential of their destructive war. During the century of their civil war the Greeks "invented full-blown political theory, thereby realizing the potential unleashed by the explosive creation of the polis as framework both for the political as a general space and for the practice of politics". At the same time, the Eleusinian Mysteries enabled the highly developed politics of Athens to keep contact and integrate the unknown mysterious forces. They allowed Athenians not to know, not to speak, only to accept the unknown as a constant in public life.

The laws derive their power from their external divine nature, but they need to be inscribed, to be constant and undeniable. There is something sacred about the act of writing; it is the voice of the unknown power of the environment that the helpless depend on without realizing it.

Theseus defends democracy by saying to the Herald:

THESEUS: . . . But when the laws are written,
The poor man and the rich have equal rights.
Then, when a wealthy citizen does wrong,
a weaker one can criticize, and prevail,
with justice on his side. That's liberty.

[426–429]

We are all equal before the law. Each subject of the polis is expected to be a separate, autonomous and mature enough individual who asks for no exemption from the law. Each one is a tragic subject responsible for forces and limits that are unknown. The agony of this fundamental asymmetry is given response by the humans struggling to institute spaces full of pleasure, meanings, feelings, and safety.

Hose (2008) understood why Zuntz – who was forced to leave Hitler's Germany in 1933 – was first to recognise the neglected political dimensions of Euripides' *Suppliants*. Theseus' praise of democracy is one of the earliest testimonies of political thinking.

Democracy ensures by the rule of law that each one is a sovereign subject. It guarantees the respect of the others towards one's narcissism. Freud (1914) and A. Freud (1965:167) observed that the human infant is a Law unto Himself, and at the same time the link of a chain to which he is bound. The parent's narcissism nestles in their love for the child. The codes of the law are not internalised in the individual's superego. What is internalised is the idea that there is a governing principle, a norm.

Theseus is not a character. He is "the symbolic representation of the city in this tragedy, which so plainly reaches out into the contemporary world of Athens" (Morwood, 2002:47). He undertakes to be the responsible subject of his fate. He harnesses himself to the yoke of necessity. Like Prometheus, he is bound by the chains of a painful process of internalisation (Potamianou, 1980). "Bound" is another key word in the play.

Theseus obeys the words of Aithra and Athena. He commits himself within the bounds of the law. He receives passively the inevitability of (internal and external) reality. He does not reject it with manic defences. Before the walls of Thebes, Theseus, the king of Athens, a shackled state, restrains himself. He retrieves the dead and leaves; he does not go on to destroy the city. By contrast, Adrastos, the king of the "stateless" state of Argos, lets himself get carried away by the excitement of the hot-headed youth and launches a destructive expedition.

We may think that the integration of a democratic polis bears the marks of the trauma of separation at its boundaries. The people abstract and separate a piece of reality from the whole unknowable world and create a separate state, differentiated, regulated by the laws. Then, like Prometheus, they enter a painful process of internalisation. After Prometheus was released, Zeus ordered him to wear a ring that was made of the steel of his chains and a piece of the rock on which he was bound. The ring of mutual recognition and belonging to the same polis keeps in its core an untranslatable "rock" of historical truth that always escapes elaboration.

The irreducible lines in ethics

Inherent in the drive is the body from whose liveliness it springs forth and the object from whose responses it acquires meaning and a raison d'etre. However, a drive retains something of the impersonal in its visceral source. It acquires meaning when it relates to the object; yet it loses something of its essence when it is elevated in relation to an object (Freud, 1905; Blass, 2016).

There is something irreducible, a grain of unelaborated perception, which did not undergo transformation and lies at the heart of every psychic formation. These grains of historical truth make the psychic constructions a necessary part of the compulsion to repeat the experiences, constantly working to negotiate the contracts of stable relationships (institutions), and construct their frames.

There is something irreducible in ethics, the responsibility towards our fellow humans. The human canon is based on the recognition that there is always the unknown that demands from us to tolerate the uncertainty, the ambiguity and the paradoxes that we meet while we try to find and create our object world. Humans live their experiences within zones of shared reality. However, the structural settings of institutions have an unyielding line which is beyond transformation. It is just what it is.

Our institutions are inventions that contain the non-dialectical chasms in the body of the society (the impossible of omnipotence) within limits (the prohibitions of the law). The laws derive their power from our shared belief that they keep at bay these basic faults, and cannot be broken without "incalculable peril" to the polis. We can think of politics in terms of the ternary logic employed by Winnicott to describe the processes of unintegration-integration-disintegration. These processes are based on the functions of a reliable maternal environment, which in a deep level holds silently the ego needs of absolute dependence and then facilitates the development of the emerging subject.

The place of Eleusis reminds us the creative potential of maternal wrath, withdraw and return. It echoes the ternary logic of unintegration-integration-disintegration of the infant's development. Hate and violence are natural in mother-infant relationship; they set limits and allow the innate creativity to be realised (Winnicott, 1960).

As long as an institution works, its settings function silently, no one knows of it. It is like the environment mother who holds the processes of transformation, without the infant knowing anything of the holding. Split-off elements need the stable frames of institutions to contain them and the poetics of politics to transform them into paradoxes, which we can tolerate inside the transitional space (Bleger, 1967; Winnicott, 1960, 1971).

A democratic polis at work, like a mother in primary maternal preoccupation, gathers elements in a dense poetic time of gestation. It gathers untranslated elements in order to gestate them and give birth to an outcome, within the bounds of the laws. The gathering place of the ancients is called agora. It is the place of assembly, exchanges, commerce and trade.

Ideal and real Athens

The protected city of the Athenians is an ideal place for the work of the rule of law, institutions, predefined rewards, and freedom of speech, poetry, history, democracy, tragedy, creation of ideas and philosophy – and doubt. This, however, is not real life. Real life is where trauma, hubris, war, epidemics, destructibility, authoritarianism, populism, and discrimination co-exist. Real life is where humans are separated violently from their loved objects and flooded with traumatic stimulation that overwhelms their ability to make sense of their lives and restore the feeling of the continuation and cohesion of their existences. In real life the forces of the good do not always win.

Theseus, the representative of the idealised democratic state, will learn to respect these forces that lie beyond reason. He learns that the logical superiority of his clever speech does not work in the real world of human suffering. He becomes aware of it by proxy through identifying and participating with sympathy, friendship and pity in the suffering of human fellow citizens and allies.

Ultimately, laws of civilization do not stop the compulsion to repeat the violence and the wars. In real life, the agony of extinction, the destruction of meaning, and the dissolution of the bonds between individuals and the city, prevail. This agony causes a fear that we have no future here any longer; we have no time or place; we will fall for ever in the abyss. Violence may erupt as a defence against this agony.

Rhem (1992:123, 130) notes that the play is set at Eleusis "home of the famous Eleusinian mysteries, the action juxtaposes the promise of spiritual rebirth with the basic human drive to bury the dead". In bacchanalian ecstasy of conjugal love, Evadne overcomes her agony of annihilation and turns the funeral pyre for her husband into a shared tomb. She dreamed of annihilation in an erotic union of their two bodies. With Evadne's self-immolation

> the waste of death becomes palpable – someone living in there before our eyes, and suddenly that someone is gone. Death, as it were is animated, revealing itself as activity, as *dying* and *killing*, rather than something mourned over as a given (the procession of dead bodies) or reported as an off-stage event (Theseus' defeat of the Thebans). The progression from death to dying proves particularly disturbing when the victim is a non-combatant, one who chooses to leave a world already awash with organized killing. . . . Evadne's suicide is not construed as a private act of grief. . . . Is a fully public act.

This is a private gesture and also a public statement; it makes personal the impersonal loss of her body. Evadne presents herself as a soldier who acts, and wins. She is not passive, she is active towards death, wants to conquer, to master the fear of loss and death. It is her father who becomes extremely passive.

> Above all, Evadne is consumed by the ideal of heroic fame. She rushes to her death "for glory's sake" . . . arrayed not in mourning but in a white dress that "means glory". . . . Her death is no doubt a product of war, but it is emphatically self-chosen, ecstatically sought and embraced as a triumph.

> (Burian, 1985:151)

Iphis' horror and his numb grief show by contrast the pathos issuing in extreme passivity. Euripides explores the inevitable compulsions to violence in this play.

Carson (2006:7–9) writes: Tragedy exists because we are full of rage, that is, full of grief. Euripides' plays shock us with their realism and extremism.

> There is in Euripides some kind of learning that is always at the boiling point. It breaks experiences open and they waste themselves, run through your fingers. Phrases don't catch them, theories don't hold them, they have no use. It is a theater of sacrifice in the true sense. Violence occurs; through violence we are intimate with some characters onstage in an exorbitant way for a brief time; that's all it is.

We can also think that Euripides imitates in his plot the repetition compulsion that gives "flesh" of reality to the ghosts of the undead. The war is an active effort to master the unsymbolised loss and kill the ghosts.

The ruthless, avenging Death-Fates, Kêres, daughters of Night, are the goddesses of inevitable violent death. They crave for blood and feast upon it after ripping the souls free from the bodies and sending them to Hades. Myriads of Kêres haunt the battlefield, like wild beasts, vultures, fighting over the dying. Some of the Kêres personify the epidemic diseases. In a few lines in the Iliad [198–202], Homer gives a powerful metaphoric dream image to describe the haunting of Hector by Achilles around the walls of Troy. The hunter cannot reach the hunted, and the hunted cannot escape the persecution. Zeus places Hector's and Achilles' respective fates, Kêres, on a golden scale. Hector's sinks to the ground.

We can think that the myth speaks of the "weight" of the uninternalised rock of reality. A nightmare starts the moment the subject dares to make a move towards internalising the lost object. He then runs to find a safe place to hide the meaning of the object he lost – and himself. The nightmare shows the difficulties that lie in the path of internalisation.

From tragedy to the "tragic", from politics to the "political"

For us, the audience, the play moves from the passions and conflicts of the plot to an open-ended process: from the tragedy to the "tragic", from the politics to the "political". The play opens up spaces. The political and the tragic remind us of the analytic object which is neither on one's nor the other's side, "but in the meeting of these two communications in the potential space which lies between them, limited by the setting". It is the transitional meeting place (Green, 1975:12).

When an episode of politics ends, we the audience leave, taking with us "a meeting place". We find ourselves in an educational arena that "reflects other paideutic spaces in Athens: the assembly, law courts, the agora, various ritual situations, schools, state funerals, performance festivities, even tragic performances as such. Adopting Lewin's formulation, these places are all "'space that matter', that build the ideological roads that connect the city within itself and out to the larger world" (Rhem, 2002:34).

Aithra rose up from her kneeling position on the orchestra floor to teach Theseus. Athena spoke down from above and taught him a lesson. Both help him to enter a path of struggle. Theseus puts himself in a regime of internalisations. He respects the unknown unconscious forces. He places himself under the yoke of necessity.

The name of Theseus etymologically is linked to "placing" (*thetein, θέτειν*), position (*thesis, θέσις*) and service (*theteia, θητεία*), the work that a slave is paid to do. To be able to perform a service has the meaning of one being capable of suffering the pain of linking love and hate together.

Such a service Prospero asked to be freed from in the end of his tragedy (Sachs, 1923). He served his time using his mysterious magic, then renounced his magic and became mortal, abandoning his omnipotence and grieving for it. Prospero could create a tragedy and attain the capacity to be mortal. He accepted the creativity of the couple, his daughter and her lover. He agreed to be in the world without omnipotent powers and with such a renouncement he, as a father, introduces his child into their polis as its subject.

Theseus achieves the capacity to perceive receptively and passively the reality which is inevitable. Courage means to have foresight. The taming of supernatural forces is part of the leader's struggle to hold the unity of the world. A service has a definite time limit that ends when the play becomes open-ended and the leader gives us immortality.

Tragedy and psychoanalysis are concerned with politics, that is, the way people struggle to be in the world. The continuing existence and the cohesion of the polis also refer to the idea of a secure agora, where words and actions weave the links of community. We, the audience of the play, give coherence to the drama, by making associations linking the internal and external reality of speech and action.

Freud (1921, 1930, 1939) established the links that make society in two movements, both meeting with resistance: One, towards unity and harmony, is based on primary identifications. The other, towards differentiation, is based on the conflict between the libidinal and destructive impulses. The driving impulses are repressed, but continue to act silently in the foundations of social links and institutions. We constantly fear that our society is on the brink of catastrophe.

Any new leader promises to rescue the unity and immortality. There is something sacred in the idea of defending the integrity of the polis, something that stems from the sacred bond uniting parent and infant. "Friendship" (*philia, φιλία*) and "pity" (*eleos, ἔλεος*) are the two elements that unite the polis according to Aristotle (2012) in his Nicomachean Ethics, (Θ, 1161a 30–35, 1161b 1–10) and in his Poetics. Friendship is the bond of mutual liking, sympathy and appreciation. Its highest form is equality, which in a political society entails freedom and autonomy (Castoriadis, 1975, 2008).

We can think that philia and eleos are based on the capacity for ego-relatedness (as opposed to id-relatedness) and the function of an environment mother (as opposed to object mother) who holds the continuity and cohesion of being (as opposed to doing, which characterises the relationships between drives and objects) (Winnicott, 1965, 1971).

The question is how to differentiate false from true friendship, which is crucial in forming a common life and future (Nehamas, 2016). Not being able to know who is a true friend, is a pathognomonic characteristic of pathological narcissism, the arrogance of hubris in politics. Denis (1982) explains that friendship bonds are based on primary and secondary autoerotic and narcissistic links (sublimated homosexuality) where we forge stable links of tenderness and the capacity to primarily and secondarily identify, and feel the position of the others.

The second element, pity, is presented in tragedy. It is not a sentimental compassion but a capacity to put oneself in the place of the other, and suffer what makes the other suffer. To be able to be in somebody else's place is a constituent of democracy. Totalitarian thinking does not recognise the other self as a different external subject that can temporally receive and exchange experiences, feelings and fantasies with the self.

Humans fight and destroy, but in the end their survival depends on their capacity to allow unconscious conflict and fantasy to work through trauma, to mourn, to think, recognise reality, and form alliances.

References

Acemoglu D. and Robinson J. (2020) *The Narrow Corridor: States, Societies and the Fate of Liberty*. New York, Penguin Books.

Aristotle's. (1996) *Poetics*. (Trans. Malcom Hearth). New York, Penguin Books.

———. (2012) *Nicomachean Ethics*. (Eds./trans. Robert C. Bartlett and Susan D. Collins). Chicago, University of Chicago Press.

Bion W. (1962 [1984]) *Learning from Experience*. London, Karnac Books.

Blass R. (2016) Understanding Freud's Conflicted View of the Object-Relatedness of Sexuality and Its Implications for Contemporary Psychoanalysis: A Re-Examination of Three Essays on the Theory of Sexuality. *International Journal of Psycho-Analysis*, *97*(3), 591–613.

Bleger J. (1967 [2013]) *Symbiosis and Ambiguity: A Psychoanalytic Study*. London, Routledge.

Burian P. (1985) Logos and Pathos: The Politics of the Suppliant Women. In P. Burian (Ed.) *Directions in Euripidean Criticism: A Collection of Essays*. Durham, NC, Duke University Press.

Carsons A. (2006) *Grief Lessons: Four Plays: Euripides*. New York, New York Review Books.

Cartledge P. (2009) *Ancient Greek Political Thought Key Themes in Ancient History*. Cambridge, Cambridge University Press.

Castoriadis C. (1975) *L' Institution imaginaire de la société*. Paris, Seuil. In Greek (Trans. S. Halikias, G. Spantidaki and K. Spantidakis, Ed. K. Soantdakis). Athens, Kedros (1981).

———. (2008) *Ce qui fait la Grece, 2. La Grece et les lois. Seminaires 1983–1984. La creation humaine III*. (Eds. E. Escobar, M. Gondicas and P. Vernay). Paris, Seuil.

Denis P. (1982 [2010]) Primary Homosexuality: A Foundation of Contradictions. In D. Briksted-Breen, S. Flandres and A. Gibeault (Eds.) *Reading French Psychoanalysis*. London and New York, Routledge.

Dimakopoulou A. (2014) *Theseus and the Moderate Democracy*. In Greek (*Euripides' the Suppliants*, Seminar 40). Athens, Koralli.

Euripides'. (1995) *Suppliant Women*. (Trans. R. Warren and S. Scully). Oxford, Oxford University Press.

Foley P. H. (1994) *The Homeric Hymn to Demeter: Translation, Commentary, and Interpretative Essays*. Princeton, Princeton University Press.

French R., Simpson P. and Harvey C. (2009) Negative Capability: A Contribution to the Understanding of Creative Leadership. In B. Sievers, et al. (Eds.) *Psychoanalytic Studies of Organizations*. London, Karnak Books.

Freud A. (1965) *Normality and Pathology in Childhood: Assessments of Development*. New York, International Universities Press.

Freud S. (1905) Three Essays on the Theory of Sexuality. *S.E., 7*.

———. (1914) On Narcissism: An Introduction. *S.E., 14*.

———. (1921) Group Psychology and the Analysis of the Ego. *S.E., 18*.

———. (1925) Negation. *S.E., 19*.

———. (1930) Civilization and Its Discontents. *S.E., 21*.

———. (1939) Moses and Monotheism. *S.E., 23*.

Green A. (1975) The Analyst, Symbolization and Absence in the Analytic Setting (On Changes in Analytic Practice and Analytic Experience). *Memory of D. W. Winnicott, International Journal of Psycho-Analysis, 56*, 1–22.

Hose M. (2008) *Euripides. Der Dichter der Leidenschaften*. Muncher, verlag C.H. Beck. In Greek (Trans. Betty Tarantili). Athens, A. Kardamitsa (2011).

Levi-Strauss C. (1922) *Tristes Tropiques*. New York, Penguin Books.

Morwood J. (2002) *The Plays of Euripides*. London, Bloomsbury.

Nehamas A. (2016) *On Friendship*. New York, Basic Books.

Nociforo N. (2017) The Invasion of Reality (or of Negotiation): The Psychoanalytic Ethic and Extinction Anxiety. *International Journal of Psycho-Analysis*, *98*, 1311–1332.

Potamianou A. (1980) Réflexions psychanalytiques sur la "Prométhia d' Eschyle" (Rapports entre l' omnipotence et la depression). In *Psychanalyse et Culture Greque. Confluents Psychanalytique*. Paris, Les Belles Lettres. In Greek (Trans. M. Fragopoulos). Athens, Rappa (1985).

Rhem R. (1992) *Greek Tragic Theatre*. London and New York, Routledge.

―――. (2002) *The Play of Space: Spatial Transformation in Greek Tragedy*. Princeton and Oxford, Princeton Universities Press.

Sachs H. (1923) The Tempest. *International Journal of Psycho-Analysis*, *4*, 43–88.

Scully S. (1995) Introduction. In *Euripides, Suppliant Women* (Trans. Rosanna Warren and Stephen Scully). Oxford, Oxford University Press.

Storey C. (2008) *Euripides: Suppliant Women*. London, Duckworth.

Winnicott D. (1960) The Theory of Parent-Infant Relationship. In *The Maturational Processes and the Facilitating Environment*. London, Karnac Books (1990).

―――. (1965) Communicating and Not Communication Leading to a Study of Certain Opposites. In *The Maturational Processes and the Facilitating Environment*. London, Karnac Books (1990).

―――. (1971) *Playing and Reality*. London, Tavistock.

6 An Ur-text of political theory

Sotiris Manolopoulos

I suggest that we, the modern audience of Euripides' *Suppliant Women*, are the future of this political play.

Euripides' *Suppliant Women* contains an Ur-text of political theory. It debates in an astonishing way that politics is a tragic process of internalisation that transforms women, men, and their city. Euripides reshapes the myth of the Suppliants into a tragic plot of the human struggles to recognise and deal with deep irreducible splits, inherent in individuals and their polis.

The tragic poet becomes a prophet and sees beyond. He reads politics as a continuous struggle to: [1] integrate split-off "wild" "supernatural" elements of human nature that lie beyond the order of politics, words, and reason, [2] form alliances of community, sustain participation in a shared reality of a common culture, [3] work through each experience so that the order of politics is reconstructed.

Politics is a transitional phenomenon in which the fundamental splits, contradictions, ruptures, and gaps of public life, are transformed into paradoxes, ambiguities, uncertainties, hesitations, semicolon syntaxes. Politics is a transitional phenomenon of culture (like art and religion). Politics uses not only words and reason but also mythical and religious acts, which are integrated into theatrical poetic metaphors. These acts give the weight of historical truth and convincing reality to the inscription of written laws and the construction of institutions.

The tragic is a psychic quality, a basic dimension of existence, a position of psychic and social development. The tragic position encompasses a separation from the primary union, an emergence of the self, the shock of loss of omnipotence and the beginning of internalisation processes.

Humans emerge from the primary union as autonomous tragic subjects who are harnessed with the yoke of necessity, that is, they undertake personally whatever will happen to them as inevitable because it has long ago been devised by mysterious unknown forces.

DOI: 10.4324/9781003252184-7

The capacity to become a tragic subject is linked with the courage to suffer and assume intrapsychic responsibility for their traumatic experiences and make them personal. It is linked with the capacity to be the thinker that can think – be a subject of – their thoughts. It is the capacity to be a suppliant, that is, to arrive at, to make one's way, to plead for the response of the object which returns the conformation of his investment.

Humans yoke themselves to – integrate, internalise, subjectivise – their drives, omnipotence and bisexuality. In *Suppliants* these necessities are manifest in the inevitability of the work of mourning and in femininity, which are interwoven in internal and external reality and lie at the foundations of psychic and public life.

The moderate democratic polis is based on the rule of law. The rule of law is based on written words, reason, and also on the historical truths of untranslated experiences that lie beyond meaning and are expressed in religion and poetry. The democratic public life is an open-ended process. The polis is constantly in transition, in crisis, and in need to reflect critically on its current state and re-invent its identity.

The development of Democracy continues in cycles of unintegration-integration-disintegration processes like individual development. Friendship and pity keep the cohesion of the polis. The subject lets the lost object die, and moves on to live among the living and inside time, ultimately becoming able to die when the time comes. In order to let the object die, the subject needs a real substitute object.

Public life is characterised by movements of omnipotent idealising fusion, painful separation, and transitional phenomena. An essential paranoia, linked to the feminine core of existence, lies at the foundations of the polis. With every movement towards integration, a paranoiac fear of attack from outside and dissolution of the polis' organisation crops up. A polis introduces the transitional phenomena of politics to help cure this acute paranoia. It is an open-ended always incomplete movement.

Politics is the struggle to innovate institutions so that they are defined by permeable boundaries, which constitute a zone of exchange. This is an area of a Third transitional reality, maintained with negations and functional transient splitting between internal and external reality. An institution consists of a capacity, a stable web of links of relationships, room where new experiences can be stored and reality can be found and constructed.

The polis consists of meeting places (agora, theatre, sanctuaries of religious rites, and feasts), where people gather to find reality, to give meaning and integrity to their polis. The human need to give meaning never dies; it endows the polis with a sense of immortality.

The institutions are defined by frames, which, like character traits, function as the bolts of irreducible splits that maintain contradictions and ruptures within a society. There, people function with positive capabilities (they know and act with certainty and clear differences), and negative capabilities (they tolerate uncertainties, ambiguities, and paradoxes). Within the bounds of institutions there are unyielding irreducible lines that lie beyond transformation. These limits are unknown in advance. This makes democracy a tragic regime.

The transitional space of the "theatrical stage" of politics links and separates the opposites, the differences. In such a "playground", everyday transferences, traumas and conflicts are expressed, interpreted by unconscious fantasies and myths (collective fantasies) and put into words. When the experiences we repeat are put into words, they acquire meaning; they are internalised. We accept responsibility for them.

Every creation of an experience is a recreation of a past one that has not been adequately represented and an anticipation of the future. Every experience is emotional, personal, and public. It is shaped, lived through, struggled with, endowed with new meanings, and internalised. We learn from it. Euripides' *Suppliant Women* can help us think of a land beyond the stage of politics that is populated by primitive untranslated elements of experience. This land has its own sensibility that poets – and psychoanalysts – try to translate.

References

Acemoglu D. and Robinson J. (2019) *The Narrow Corridor: States, Societies and the Fate of Liberty*. New York, Penguin Books.
Aisenstein M. (2017) *An Analytic Journey: From the Art of Archery to the Art of Psychoanalysis*. London, Karnac.
———. (2019) *Desir-Douleur-Pensee*. In Greek (Trans. S. Leonidi, Ed. P. Aloupis). Athens, Agra Publications.
Arendt H. (1958) *The Human Condition*. Chicago, The University of Chicago Press.
———. (1979) *The Origins of Totalitarianism*. New York, Harcourt Brace Jovanovich.
Aristotle's. (1996) *Poetics*. (Trans. Malcom Hearth). New York, Penguin Books.
———. (2012) *Nicomachean Ethics*. (Eds./trans. Robert C. Bartlett, and Susan D. Collins). Chicago, The University of Chicago Press.
Arvanitakis K. (1998) Some Thoughts on the Essence of the Tragic. *International Journal of Psycho-Analysis*, *79*(5), 955–964.
Aulagnier P. (1975 [2001]) *The Violence of Interpretation: From Pictogram to Statement*. London and New York, Routledge.
Bell D. (2007) Psychoanalytic Perspectives on the Dionysiac and the Apollonian in Euripides's Bacchae. In C. Bainbridge et. al. (Eds.) *Culture and the Unconscious*. Basingstoke, UK, Palgrave MacMillan.
Bick E. (1968) The Experience of the Skin in Early Object-Relations. *International Journal of Psycho-Analysis*, *49*, 484–486.
Bion W. (1961) *Experiences in Groups and Other Papers*. London, Tavistock.
———. (1962 [1984]) *Learning from Experience*. London, Karnac Books.
———. (1965 [1984]) *Transformations*. London, Karnac Books.
Blass R. (2016) Understanding Freud's Conflicted View of the Object-Relatedness of Sexuality and Its Implications for Contemporary Psychoanalysis: A Re-Examination of Three Essays on the Theory of Sexuality. *International Journal of Psycho-Analysis*, *97*(3), 591–613.
Bleger J. (1967 [2013]) *Symbiosis and Ambiguity: A Psychoanalytic Study*. London, Routledge.
Breen D. (1993) *The Gender Conundrum: Contemporary Psychoanalytic Perspectives on Femininity and Masculinity*. (Ed. and Intro. Dana Breen). Hove and New York, Brunner-Routledge.

Burian P. (1985) Logos and Pathos: The Politics of the Suppliant Women. In P. Burian (Ed.) *Directions in Euripidean Criticism: A Collection of Essays*. Durham, NC, Duke University Press.

Cambridge University Press, Faculty of Classics. (2021) *The Cambridge Greek Lexicon*. Vol. 1. & 2. Cambridge, Cambridge University Press.

Castoriadis C. (1975) *L'Institution imaginaire de la société*. Paris, Editions du Seuil. In Greek (Trans. S. Halikias, G. Spantidaki and K. Spantidakis, Ed. K. Soantdakis). Athens, Kedros (1981).

———. (1999) *The Ancient Greek Democracy and Its Significance for Us Today*. In Greek. Athens, Ypsilon.

———. (2008) *Ce qui fait la Grece, 2. La Grece et les lois. Seminaires 1983–1984. La creation humaine III*. (Eds. E. Escobar, M. Gondicas and P. Vernay). Paris, Editions du Seuil.

Chabert C. (2019) Plural Feminine: Hysteria, Masochism or Melancholia? *International Journal of Psycho-Analysis*, *100*(3), 584–592.

Denis P. (1982 [2010]) Primary Homosexuality: A Foundation of Contradictions. In D. Briksted-Breen, S. Flandres and A. Gibeault (Eds.) *Reading French Psychoanalysis*. London and New York, Routledge.

De Romilly J. (1971) *Le Temps dans la Tragedie Grecque*. Paris, VRIN.

Devereux G. (1981) *Baubo, la vulve mythique*. Paris, Payot. In Greek. Athens, Olkos (1997).

Dimakopoulou A. (2014) *Theseus and the Moderate Democracy*. In Greek (*Euripides' The Suppliants*, Seminar 40). Athens, Koralli.

Euripides'. (1995) *Suppliant Women*. (Trans. R. Warren and S. Scully). Oxford, Oxford University Press.

Ferenczi S. (1933 [1955]) The Confusion of Tongues Between Adults and the Child: The Language of Tenderness and of Passion. In E. Mosbacher, et al. (Trans.) *Final Contributions to the Problems and Methods of Psychoanalysis*. London, Maresfield Reprints.

Foley P. (1985) *Ritual Irony: Poetry and Sacrifice in Euripides*. Ithaca and London, Cornell University Press.

French R., Simpson P. and Harvey C. (2009) Negative Capability: A Contribution to the Understanding of Creative Leadership. In B. Sievers, et al. (Eds.) *Psychoanalytic Studies of Organizations*. London, Karnak Books.

Freud A. (1965) *Normality and Pathology in Childhood: Assessments of Development*. New York, International Universities Press.

Freud S. (1895 [1950]) Project for a Scientific Psychology. *S.E., 1*. – Letter to Wilhelm Fliess of 15th October 1897: Letter 71. In (Trans. E. Mosbacher and J. Strackey) *The Origins of Psycho-Analysis: Letters to Wilhelm Fliess, Drafts and Notes, 1887–1902*. London, Imago (1954).

———. (1901) The Psychology of Everyday Life. *S.E., 6*.

———. (1905) Three Essays on the Theory of Sexuality, *S.E., 7*.

———. (1912–1913) Totem and Taboo: Some Points of Agreement between the Mental Lives of Savages and Neurotics. *S.E., 13*.

———. (1913) The Theme of Three Caskets. *S.E., 13*.

————. (1914) On Narcissism. An Introduction. *S.E.*, *14*.

————. (1915) Instincts and their Vicissitudes. *S.E.*, *14*.

————. (1915 [1917]) Mourning and Melancholia. *S.E.*, *14*.

————. (1916–1917) Introductory Lectures on Psycho-Analysis. *S.E.*, *14*.

————. (1919) The Uncanny. *S.E.*, *17*.

————. (1920) Beyond the Pleasure Principle. *S.E.*, *18*.

————. (1921) Group Psychology and the Analysis of the Ego. *S.E.*, *18*.

————. (1925) Negation. *S.E.*, *19*.

————. (1930) Civilization and its Discontents. *S.E.*, *21*.

————. (1937a) Analysis Terminable and Interminable. *S.E.*, *23*.

————. (1937b) Constructions in Analysis. *S.E.*, *23*.

————. (1939) Moses and Monotheism. *S.E.*, *23*.

————. (1940a) An Outline of Psychoanalysis. *S.E.*, *23*.

————. (1940b) Splitting of the Ego in the Process of Defence. *S.E.*, *23*.

Green A. (1972) Aggression, Femininity, Paranoia and Reality. *International Journal of Psycho-Analyis*, *53*, 205–211.

————. (1975) The Analyst, Symbolization and Absence in the Analytic Setting (On Changes in Analytic Practice and Analytic Experience). In *Memory of D. W. Winnicott, International Journal of Psycho-Analysis*, *56*, 1–22.

————. (1980) Thésée et Oedipe. Une iterprétation psychanalytique de la Théséide. In *Psychanalyse et Culture Greque. Confluents Psychanalytique*. Paris, Les Belles Lettres. In Greek (Trans. M. Fragopoulos). Athens, Ekdoseis Rappa (1985).

————. (1991) *Narcissism de vie, narcissism de mort*. Paris, Éditions de Minuit. English trans. *Life Narcissism, Death Narcissism*. (Trans. A. Weller). London, Free Association Books (2001).

Grube G. (1941) *The Drama of Euripides*. London, Methuen.

Hamilton E. (1930 [2017]) *The Greek Way*. New York, W.W. Norton & Company.

Harrison J. (1903 [1992]) *Prolegomena to the Study of Greek Religion*. Princeton, New Jersey, Princeton University Press. In Greek (Trans. E. Papadopoulou). Athens, Iamvlihos (1996).

Hartocollis P. (1983) *Time and Timelessness*. New York, International Universities Press.

Jouanna D. (2015) *Les Greecs aux Enfers. D' Homère a Épicure*. Paris, Les Belles Lettres. In Greek (Trans. H. Magoulas, Ed. S. Metevelis). Athens, Estia (2019).

Kaës R. (2007) *Linking, Alliances and Shared Space: Groups and the Psychoanalyst*. London, The International Psychoanalytic Library.

Kitto H. (1961) *Greek Tragedy*. London and New York, Routledge.

Knox B. (1985) Euripides: The Poet as Prophet. In P. Burian (Ed.) *Directions in Euripidean Criticism: A Collection of Essays*. Durham, Duke University Press.

Kovacs D. (1998) *Euripides: Suppliant Women, Electra, Heracles*. Cambridge, MA, Harvard University Press.

Kristeva J. (2000 [2007]) From Symbols to Flesh: The Polymorphous Destiny of Narration. In P. Williams and G. Gabbard (Eds.) *Key Papers in Literature and Psychoanalysis*. London, Karnac Books.

Levi-Strauss C. (1922) *Tristes Tropiques*. New York, Penguin Books.

Loraux N. (1986) *The Invention of Athens: The Funeral Oration in the Classical City*. Cambridge, MA, Harvard University Press.

———. (1987) *Tragic Ways of Killing a Woman*. Cambridege, MA, Harvard Universities Press.

———. (2002) *The Mourning Voice: An Essay on Greek Tragedy*. London, Cornell University Press.

Manolopoulos S. (1999) 'Euripides' Hippolytus: The Familiar Things. *Psychoanalytic Studies*, *1*(2), 177–189.

———. (2003) The Sense of Transience in Transferential and Transitional Phenomena. *Israel Psychoanalytic Journal*, *1*(2), 225–245.

———. (2015) Medea by Euripides: Psychic Constructions for Preverbal Experiences and Traumas. *The Psychoanalytic Quarterly*, *84*(2), 441–461.

———. (2016) Discussion of Michael Parsons' Paper. *Psychoanalyis in Europe, EPF Bulletin*, *70*, 29–34.

March J. (1990) Euripides the Misogynist? In A. Powel (Ed.) *Euripides, Women and Sexuality*. London and New York, Routledge.

Mendelshon D. (2002) *Gender and the City in Euripides' Political Plays*. New York, Oxford Universitiy Press.

Morwood J. (2002) *The Plays of Euripides*. London, Bloomsbury.

Nehamas A. (2016) *On Friendeship*. New York, Basic Books.

Nociforo N. (2017) The Invasion of Reality (or of Negotiation): The Psychoanalytic Ethic and Extinction Anxiety. *International Journal of Psycho-Analysis*, *98*, 1311–1332.

Ogden T. (2002) A New Reading of the Origins of Object-Relations Theory. *International Journal of Psycho-Analysis*, *83*(4), 767–782.

———. (2004) The Analytic Third: Implications for Psychoanalytic Theory and Technique. *Psychoanalytic Quarterly*, *73*, 67–195.

Parsons M. (1990) Self-knowledge Refused and Accepted. *Journal of Analytic Psychology*, *35*(1), 19–40.

———. (2014) Why Did Orpheus Look Back? Après-coup, avant-coup. In *Living Psychoanalysis*. London and New York, Routledge.

———. (2016) Authors of our own Authority. *Psychoanalyis in Europe, EPF Bulletin*, *70*, 19–28.

Petrou A. (2019) Mother's Primacy in Anthropology and Psychoanalysis. *Romanian Journal of Psychoanalysis*, *12*(2), 70–92.

Plutarch's. (1993) *Lives, Theseus and Romulus, Lycurgus and Numa, Solon and Publicola*. (Trans. B. Perrin). Cambridge, MA, Harvard University Press.

Potamianou A. (1980) Réflexions psychanalytiques sur la "Prométhia d' Eschyle" (Rapports entre l' omnipotence et la depression). In *Psychanalyse et Culture Greque. Confluents Psychanalytique*. Paris, Les Belles Lettres. In Greek (Trans. M. Fragopoulos). Athens, Rappa (1985).

———. (1996) *Hope: A Shield in the Economy of Borderline States*. London and New York, Routledge.

Rich A. (1986 [1995]) *Of Woman Born: Motherhood as Experience and Institution*. New York, Norton.

Rhem R. (1992) *Greek Tragic Theatre*. London and New York, Routledge.

———. (2002) *The Play of Space: Spatial Transformation in Greek Tragedy*. Princeton and Oxford, Princeton Universities Press.

Rose J. (2018) *Mothers. An Essay on Love and Cruelty*. London, Faber & Faber.

Rosenfeld H. (1971) A Clinical Approach to the Psychoanalytic Theory of the Life and Death Instincts: An Investigation into the Aggressive Aspects of Narcissism. *International Journal of Psycho-Analysis*, *52*, 169–178.

Sachs H. (1923) The Tempest. *International Journal of Psycho-Analysis*, *4*, 43–88.

Scarfone D. (2011) Repetition: Between Presence and Meaning. *Canadian Journal of Psychoanalysis*, *19*(1), 70–86.

Sklar J. (2018) *Dark Times: Psychoanalytic Perspectives on Politics, History, and Mourning*. London, Phoenix Publishing House.

Seferis G. (1995) II Mycenae, Oct. 1935. In *George Seferis Complete Poems* (Trans. E. Keeley and P. Sherrard). London. Carcanet Classics.

Steiner R. (2007) Does the Pierce's Semiotic Model Based on Index, Icon, Symbol Have Anything to do with Psychoanalysis? In G. Ambrosio, S. Argentieri and J. Canestri (Eds.) *Language, Symboliszation, and Psychosis: Essays in Honour of Jacqueline Amati Mehler*. London, Karnac.

Storey C. (2008) *Euripides: Suppliant Women*. London, Duckworth.

Suljagic J. (2016) The Many Facets of Authority in Psychoanalytic Institutions (unpublished paper). Available at: www.epf-fep.eu/eng/article/the-many-facets-of-authority-in-psychoanalytic-institutions (requires login).

Thucydides'. (1910) *The Peloponnesian War*. London, J. M. Dent; New York, E. P. Dutton. Available at: www.perseus.tufts.edu/hopper/text?doc=Perseus%3Atext%3A1999.01.0200%3Abook%3D2%3Achapter%3D47

Tustin F. (1986) *Autistic Barriers in Neurotic Patients*. London, Karnac Books.

Wilkins J. (1990) The State and the Individual: Euripides' Plays of Voluntary Self-Sacrifice. In A. Powel (Ed.) *Euripides, Women and Sexuality*. London and New York, Routledge.

Williams B. (1947 [1992]) *Hate in Countertransference: Through Paediatrics to Psycho-Analysis*. London, Karnac Books.

———. (1948 [1992]) Reparation in Respect of Mother's Organized Defence Against Depression. In *Through Paediatrics to Psychoanalysis*. London, Karnac Books.

———. (1960 [1990]) The Theory of Parent-Infant Relationship. In *The Maturational Processes and the Facilitating Environment*. London, Karnac Books.

———. (1963a [1990]) The Development of the Capacity for Concern. In *The Maturational Processes and the Facilitating Environment*. London, Karnac Books.

———. (1963b [1990]) Morals and Education. In *The Maturational Processes and the Facilitating Environment*. London, Karnac Books.

———. (1965 [1990]) Communicating and Not Communication Leading to a Study of Certain Opposites. In *The Maturational Processes and the Facilitating Environment*. London, Karnac Books.

———. (1971) *Playing and Reality*. London, Tavistock.

———. (1974) The Fear of Breakdown. *International Review of Psychoanalysis*, *1*, 103–107.

———. (1980) *Home Is Where we Start From: Essays By a Psychoanalyst*. New York, Penguin Books.

———. (1988) *Human Nature*. London, Free Association Books.

———. (1993) *Shame and Necessity*. Berkeley and Los Angeles, University of California Press.

Zeitlin F. (1996) *Playing the Other: Gender and Society in Classical Greek Literature*. Chicago and London, The University of Chicago Press.

Zunt G. (1955) *The Political Plays of Euripides*. Manchester, Manchester University Press.

Index

108   *Index*

Eteokles 4

Eumenides, The 37–38

Euripides 1–2; on Aeschylean justice
39; *Bacchae* 51; *Children of
Herakles* 14, 16; contradictions and
surprises used by 17, 28; epidemic
in Athens and 15; everyday familiar
speech used by 16; *Suppliant
Women (see Suppliant Women)*; as
tragedy writer 16–17; use of women
characters by 56–57

Evadne 10–11, 16, 17, 58, 65, 73;
Eleusinian promise and 67–68; self-
immolation by 65–66, 92; as tragic
symbol 71–72; united with primary
object 69

extinction, fear of 87–88

fear of extinction 87–88

femininity: birth and war and 77–79;
disruptive otherness of 69–70;
Eleusinian promise and 67–68;
fear of 56; fire of madness in
70–72; freedom and 64–65, 68;
identification with 64–65; matriarchy
in Athens and 57–58; mysteries of
58–60; paranoia linked to 72–73;
primary creativity in 60–61; sacrifice
in 65–66, 68; split elements of 58;
Suppliants space of mourning and
62–64; tension between harmony
of union and differentiation of
autonomy in 68–69; Thesmoforia
and 75–76; tragic symbolism of
71–72; of two deities 74–75

Ferenczi, S. 30

Foley, P. H. 38, 66

freedom 64–65, 68, 79

Freud, A. 89

Freud, S. 2, 19, 28, 30, 57, 77, 89, 94

friendship 95, 99

funeral orations 26–27, 36, 42, 49, 57

Green, A. 17, 49, 64

Grube, G. 16

Harrison, J. 75

Herakles 12, 73

Hitler, A. 53, 89

Homer 7, 24, 41

Hose, M. 89

hubris 9–10, 29–30, 85, 86–87

idealised democratic state 91–93

immortality 49–50, 52

integration processes 52

intellect 23–25

Iphis 10–11, 42, 56, 66, 93

irreducible in ethics, the 90–91

justice 7

Kaës, R. 29

Kitto, H. 16

Klein, M. 19, 52

Knox, B. 17

koinonia 10, 42

Kore 4–5, 44, 63, 71, 74

Lévi-Strauss, C. 85

logos 17–18, 25; constructing meaning
30

Loraux, N. 27, 35, 68, 71

matriarchy 57–58

melting 68

Mendelshon, D. 56–57, 63, 69–70, 71,
73

mother-child relationship 19–20,
30–31; core of primary femininity in
58–59; ethics originating in 59; fire
of madness in 70–72; freedom and
65; *see also* children

mourning: bringing the future 41–43;
funeral orations in 26–27, 36, 42,
49, 57; idealising the dead in 36;
linear time and separation in 47–49;
opening the space of the agora
43–44; participation in social life
and 52–53; as public affair 36, 40,
62–64; rescuing the dead 36–38;
rules on 35–36; space of 62–64; split
between fear and confidence 38–39;
weight of 45–47; *see also* death

myths, reality in 22–23, 50–51

narcissistic contract 28–29

necessity 7; of war 8–10

negation 84

non-verbal signs 19

For Product Safety Concerns and Information please contact our EU
representative GPSR@taylorandfrancis.com Taylor & Francis Verlag GmbH,
Kaufingerstraße 24, 80331 München, Germany

Printed and bound by CPI Group (UK) Ltd, Croydon, CR0 4YY
11/04/2025
01844010-0005